Yankee

COLORS

Yankee
COLORS

The GLORY YEARS *of the* MANTLE ERA

Photographs by
MARVIN E. NEWMAN

Text by
AL SILVERMAN

Foreword by
YOGI BERRA

Edited by
CHRISTOPHER SWEET

Editor: Rebecca Isenberg
Art Director: Michelle Ishay
Designer: José A. Contreras
Production Manager: Alison Gervais

Library of Congress Cataloging-in-Publication Data

Silverman, Al.
 Yankee colors : the glory years of the Mantle era /
photographs by Marvin E. Newman ; text by Al Silverman;
foreword by Yogi Berra.
    p. cm.
 ISBN 978-0-8109-9638-0 (Harry N. Abrams, inc.)
 1. New York Yankees (Baseball team)—History—20th century.
I. Title.

GV875.N4S56 2009
796.357′64097471—dc22

                     2008039387

Photographs copyright © 2009 Marvin E. Newman
Text copyright © 2009 Al Silverman

Printed and bound in China
10 9 8 7 6 5 4 3 2 1

Abrams books are available at special discounts when
purchased in quantity for premiums and promotions as
well as fundraising or educational use. Special editions
can also be created to specification. For details, contact
specialmarkets@hnabooks.com or the address below.

harry n. abrams, inc.
a subsidiary of La Martinière Groupe

115 West 18th Street
New York, NY 10011
www.hnabooks.com

Contents

Foreword
by Yogi Berra

Sometimes in baseball you don't know nothing. You don't know what surprises lie ahead. But it's still the greatest game and I got to play in one of the greatest eras. Looking back, that era seems almost prehistoric. Games were in the afternoon. There was no Internet. Television was still new. We traveled by train. People took subways to the World Series. Players lived in the same neighborhoods as fans.

We weren't rich but we had a great team spirit on the Yankees. And we had some fun. Playing in 14 World Series in 17 seasons, that wasn't too bad. I was just born at the right time.

Now people always ask if I'll miss Yankee Stadium or how I feel about the new one. What can I say? Buildings aren't forever. What is forever are the memories because they live inside you. So I don't get too sentimental over this stadium business, especially after they remodeled it in the 1970s. It wasn't really the same place we played. We played in the Yankee Stadium that had Death Valley, 461 feet to left-center, the stone monuments in center field, and all those championship banners hanging from the roof. That place was an original, like an old cathedral. It was bigger, grander than anything imaginable. It had a lot of greatness considering it was the place built for Babe Ruth, and he helped the Yankees become the Yankees.

I can't forget my memories there. Our Yankee teams were real close-knit and the stadium was like our home. It's where I was lucky enough to play on 10 championship teams. Great things happened there. You put on the pinstripes, it's expected you do pretty good.

When I first joined the Yankees over sixty years ago, I looked around the clubhouse and saw DiMaggio, Henrich, Keller, Rizzuto. You saw those guys and you felt the pride and responsibility in what it meant being a Yankee. In the beginning some people said I didn't belong. They said I didn't even look like a Yankee, let alone a regular ballplayer. Well, as a catcher I was terrible. After my second season, the Yankees brought Bill Dickey out of retirement to help me—or learn me all his experience as I said. That was part of the Yankee tradition, somebody helping somebody. And Bill was one of the greatest ever and played with some of the greatest. He was a teammate of Ruth and Gehrig. And he patiently worked on me to help me become the catcher I became. Every year I still go to spring training and try to help if I can. It's part of Yankee tradition.

Another is Old Timers' Day. No team but the Yankees does it anymore. It's a wonderful day. All those guys, newer older guys and the real old ones like me, coming back to Yankee Stadium. Even the guys playing today, Jeter, Rivera, Posada—we all have that lifetime bond, being Yankees and playing in the greatest place you can play. Of course, Yankee Stadium has changed and it's changing again. But one thing that doesn't change is the memories. The great photos in this great book bring them back—memories you can't forget.

Mickey Mantle and Casey Stengel, 1956, the year Mantle won baseball's Triple Crown (he led the major leagues with a batting average of .353, the most home runs at 52, and the most RBIs at 130) and his first of three MVP awards.

The Great Yankee Dynasty

by Al Silverman

CASEY AND THE MICK

I wondered what the brand-new manager of the New York Yankees was thinking about that opening day of April 19, 1949, when, in a pregame ceremony held in deepest center field at Yankee Stadium, Casey Stengel watched the granite monument to Babe Ruth—the Yankees' first unveiling in its history—set into its sacred place. Along with Ruth, two other Yankees were honored with plaques: one to Lou Gehrig, the other to Miller Huggins, the first grand-master manager the Yankees ever had. My guess is that Casey was probably fretting about Huggins lying there next to the Babe and hoping he would be squeezed in some day.

You have to think of Casey Stengel that way. Once, when asked who was the best manager he had ever seen, Casey said simply, "I was the best manager I ever saw, and I tell people that to shut 'em up. And also because I believe it."

Not me. Back in the Boston area where I grew up, I hated Casey Stengel for what he had done with my favorite team of my young life, the Boston Braves. Dave Egan, the leading sports columnist among the Boston newspapers, got it right in 1943 after Stengel was hit by a taxi and broke his leg. Egan, noted for his whimsical opinions, called on his constituents to honor the driver who had whacked Stengel by voting for him as "the man who had done the most for baseball in Boston that year."

It got so bad for the Braves that one year they were actually given the nickname of the Bees. In his six Boston years, Stengel buzzed the team to one fifth-place finish, one sixth-place finish and—*shudder*—four years in seventh place. If you were a Dodger fan you had to endure just three years with him; the results were similar. How then did the Yankees decide that the fifty-eight-year-old Stengel should become their keeper?

It was George Weiss, the Yankees' cunning general manager, in those years the Talleyrand of baseball, who prevailed on the top brass to give his friend Stengel a two-year contract. It needn't be a big-money deal, Weiss knew, because Stengel and his wife Edna were in the money, having earned millions from their investments in oil. Also, Stengel had just come through a winning season, managing Oakland to a pennant in the Pacific Coast League. What did the Yankees have to lose? They were in transition anyway, shedding elderly players they once loved and looking to hurry the futures of some great-looking youngsters in their farm system. So they figured Casey Stengel, who was also a schoolteacher at heart, would be the guy to handle a franchise in flux. Leave it to Ed Linn, a probing writer on sports in his time, to sum it up best: "He spent the best years of his middle age as a second-division manager," Linn said of Stengel, "and the best years of his old age as the most successful manager of all time."

Mickey Mantle, 1955.

In 1957 Marvin Newman and I were unwashed children of the 1950s, when we decided to become magazine publishers.

How was this possible? At the time I was simply a freelance writer for magazines, most of which you've never heard of: *Real, Men, See, Swank, Nugget*. And Marvin Newman, who was already gaining a reputation as a sports photographer of note, had come to understand that, for him, photography was art, and in that direction he went.

In the spring training season of 1953, Marvin was assigned by *Sport* magazine (I was on their staff then, learning how to be an editor) to go down to St. Petersburg, Florida, then the home of the Yankees, to shoot the players but to concentrate on Mickey Mantle, even though he was still a hero in the making.

It was great for Marvin hanging out with Mickey and a lot of his teammates. He even got to meet Casey Stengel up close. For the first time, photographers covering the game in the preseason were allowed to go on the field. During one game, Marvin found himself shooting while crouched between first base and home. The manager, Old Perfesser Stengel, immediately stopped the action and pulled Marvin over to him. "Look, kid," he said, "if you're really going to take pictures on the field, you better put on a helmet." Marvin did and went back to work.

The Yankees' training field was right next to the stadium. So when the workouts were over Mick and Marv would lie on the grass together and just talk. Marv also remembers the time when Mickey "borrowed" a huge tractor in the field (Marvin provides proof on page 28) and drove hither and yon showing how they did it in Commerce, Oklahoma. "Mickey would tell me about his family back in Commerce," Marv said, "but he also wanted to know from me what New York was really like for someone who had lived there all his life." He particularly liked asking Marvin about the girls of New York because he sensed that Marvin was an expert on the subject. That was possible.

When Mickey first came to New York he lived for awhile in the Bronx with other bachelor Yankees at the huge, fancy Concourse Plaza Hotel, which was a trot down to Yankee Stadium. I was fascinated to learn that the Concourse Plaza had been dedicated in October 1923, just about the time that Casey Stengel, who was then playing the outfield for John McGraw's New York Giants, had won 2 World Series games for the Giants with 2 home runs. The Yankees, however, who were playing their first World Series in their brand-new ballpark—"the House that Ruth built"—went on to win their first world championship. And Dynasty I was in the works.

Mickey abandoned the Concourse Plaza as soon as possible and became a city boy on his own. He may have inherited some sophistication from his photographer friend. On the other hand, he roomed with Billy Martin for a period of time, and it is well known that Billy taught Mickey a lot more than Marvin ever could.

It was when Mantle's career exploded in 1956—he won the vaunted Triple Crown that year, which means he led the league in batting, .353; in home runs, 52; and in runs batted in, 130—that Marvin came to me.

"Al," he said, "why don't we do a one-shot magazine just on Mickey?" I wasn't sure that it would work—a whole issue of a magazine on one person? We were both still ducklings, plus where would we get the money? But I told him, "Let's do it." We did manage to find investors, mostly from understanding people in our families. And Marvin made a deal to get Mickey's backing, and this greeting on the first page:

To My Fans—Best Wishes
Mickey Mantle

Working so closely with Marvin Newman on this book, he loosened up, decided to tell me the secret he had held onto for half a century—the real reason he wanted to do the Mantle one-shot. Back then he was sharing a studio with a bunch of photographers, including one Al Wertheimer. Wertheimer had just done his own one-shot on a young singer he had photographed all by himself thousands of times—Elvis Presley. Wertheimer sold 400,000 copies of that magazine. Mickey, who could hardly sing a note, was no competition. Still, Marvin and I ended up managing a small profit for us and our investors.

That 1953 experience of being around a team like the Yankees, baseball's most glorious institution, did wonders for our photographer. He was also working on assignment for a magazine that would make its debut in 1954: *Sports Illustrated,* they would call it. So Marvin came back from Florida not only as a sports photographer on the rise, but also as a youngster who had found himself a lifelong friend in Mickey Mantle. That would enable him to enjoy the company of many of the other players, whose careers had begun shaping what came to be the Yankees' greatest dynasty.

DIMAG

It used to be that the Baseball Writers of America always voted in the preseason on which teams had the best prospects for success that year. In 1949, the Boston Red Sox led the pack with 118 votes. The Cleveland Indians finished second with 79 votes. Casey Stengel's Yankees got 6 votes. (It wouldn't be until Stengel's fifth year on the job that the baseball writers would make peace with the Yankees, by voting for them to win it all.)

In 1949, Stengel's rookie year, all sorts of things were happening to cause discomfort among the Yankee players as well as their fans, not the least of which was their new manager's way of doing business. Joe McCarthy, in his successful sixteen years as the Yankee manager, was called by some "a pushbutton manager." His players did have to follow some strict rules, including wearing jackets and ties at hotel breakfasts. On the other hand, each player had a position to play; it was his if he played it well. When, for instance, Tommy Henrich trotted out, it was always to right field. In '49, under Stengel, Henrich trotted to both first base and right field. With Casey Stengel, everything was up for grabs as he installed a rigid platoon system.

In 1948, George "Snuffy" Stirnweiss played second base. In 1949, Stengel had rookie Jerry Coleman share second base with Stirnweiss. In 1948, Billy Johnson played third base. In 1949, he played against left-handed pitchers, and Bobby Brown, the other third baseman, played against right-handers. It wasn't just that. "When we needed a long fly to get a man from third," Jerry Coleman said, "Casey sent Joe Collins up (the Yankees' first baseman) to hit for me. It was the right move because I knew Collins, a slugger, had a much better chance of hitting that fly than I did."

In the outfield, Johnny Lindell played left field in '48, but in '49 when the Yankees picked up Gene Woodling in a trade, he became the left fielder—most of the time. Neither Lindell nor Woodling was happy to be a part-timer. "Naturally, I want to play all the time," Woodling told a writer for *Sport* magazine. "What kind of a ballplayer would I be if I conceded that I couldn't hit left-handers.

Mickey Mantle going up to bat at Yankee Stadium, 1956. Hank Bauer is to the right in the dugout.

On the other hand I always said that from Casey's point of view, he was getting a hitter as good as me, and maybe even better, and he was getting the lefty-righty percentage he wanted."

The problem for the Yankees in 1949 was not the Stengel platoon system as it began to unfold, but an epidemic of injuries, none worse than the one that kept Joe DiMaggio out of the lineup in the team's first 65 games. It also froze the relationship between DiMaggio and Stengel that lasted until DiMaggio's retirement after the 1951 season.

The Yankee Clipper was no kid anymore. He had been with the Yankees since 1936, not counting the three years he spent in World War II. He was approaching thirty-five, beginning to feel physical afflictions in his shoulders, elbows, legs, and knees. Yet in 1948 he enjoyed one of his most brilliant years. He batted .320 and led the league with 39 home runs and 155 runs batted in. In most of his 153 games he played in pain.

In November of '46, DiMaggio had been operated on for a bone spur on his left heel. It caused him trouble early in the '47 season, but he played through the pain. Then, in November of '48, he had surgery for a new spur on his right heel. It didn't work. Joe told his friends that it felt "like an ice pick was stabbing me." He went back to Johns Hopkins in Baltimore for another examination. The doctors said that he now had broken adhesions in the

Joe DiMaggio, the "Yankee Clipper," takes the field at Yankee Stadium on Old Timers' Day, August 1978.

foot. There was nothing to be done about it. Eventually, it would cure itself.

In April of '49 his foot became inflamed. Back at Johns Hopkins the doctors treated an infection and told him again that the pain would eventually go away. Only they didn't know when.

One morning, at the end of June, DiMaggio awoke and did his customary routine: he put his bad foot on the floor, anticipating the usual pain. But this time he felt no pain. DiMag stood up, walked around, felt his heel—it was not hot. His Yankees were on the road but that was okay with Joe. He got ex-ballplayer friends to help him work out at the stadium. Someone threw baseballs at him and he sprayed them all over the outfield and, more than a few of them, into the stands, quitting only when the blisters he had grew bloody.

Next for the Yankees would be a three-game series against the Red Sox in Fenway Park. The team took the train to Boston, but Joe stayed back; he wasn't sure that he was ready to play. But it was a night game, and by mid-afternoon he had changed his mind and took a plane to Boston. He dressed, but said nothing to Stengel. Just before the game started, he told Stengel he would

try playing. Stengel immediately penciled DiMaggio into the lineup.

The Yankees were leading the league, but the Red Sox were not far behind them. Allie Reynolds was the Yankees' starting pitcher and Mickey McDermott, a youngster with a blazing fastball, was starting for Boston. DiMaggio's first time up he singled. Red Sox fans that filled Fenway Park began to feel nervous. Was the Yankees' DiMaggio (the Sox had their own DiMaggio, center fielder Dominic DiMaggio) really feeling better? Joe showed them. His second time up he hit a home run into the screen atop Boston's "Green Monster" in left field. The Yankees won the game, 5–4.

The next day the Yankees' erratic left-hander, Tommy Byrne, was routed by the Sox, who took a 7–1 lead into the fifth inning. Joe DiMaggio came up with Phil Rizzuto and Tommy Henrich on base, and blasted a three-run home run. That made it 7–4, Boston. In the eighth, DiMaggio came up with a man on base. This time he hit one *over* the Green Monster, his second homer of the game, his third of the series. In his powerful biography, *Joe DiMaggio: The Hero's Life*, Richard Ben Cramer described the scene as DiMaggio rounded the bases: "As Joe touched home plate and turned toward the dugout, Stengel emerged, hands high in the air. Then he backed away as Joe approached, bowing and salaaming to the potentate."

That was probably the high note in the relationship between the manager and his ace ballplayer.

The pennant race was still too close to call. It came down to the last game of the year, with the Red Sox and Yankees still clinging to the pennant raft. The Yankees won it, 5–3. They would face the Brooklyn Dodgers in the World Series.

It was the Dodgers of Jackie Robinson and Pee Wee Reese—the Dodgers who would later become "the Boys of Summer," but not this summer. The Yankees beat them in five games, giving Casey Stengel his first world championship.

The Cinderella year for Joe DiMaggio was over.

In 1950 Casey Stengel vowed not to pander to the Yankees' greatest player since Babe Ruth. It didn't help that Joe wasn't hitting. On June 21 he did reach a highpoint in his career when he got his 2,000th hit. But he kept slipping. Then, on August 11, his batting average down to .279, with only 4 hits in his last 38 times up, Stengel benched him.

DiMaggio sat out for six games. It would have been longer but outfielder Hank Bauer was beaned sliding into third base and had to leave the lineup. So Joe DiMaggio was back in center field. Casey Stengel got lucky because DiMaggio went on a tear that would make the world right again for him. Over the next six weeks Joe batted .376 with 11 home runs. He had returned just in time to help the Yankees beat out the Detroit Tigers and win a second pennant for Stengel.

DiMaggio ended the season with respectable stats—a .301 batting average, 32 home runs, 122 RBIs.

The World Series was a lark for the Yankees. They took four straight from the Philadelphia Phillies' "Whiz Kids."

After the last series' game, Stengel, munching on crow, went over to DiMaggio who was resting by his locker. "Joe," he said, "we couldn't have done it without you."

In 1964, *Sport* magazine did an engaging story: "The Greatest Center Fielder Ever" as chosen by the living Hall of Famers. When the votes were all in it was a tie between Tris Speaker, the amazing center fielder for the pre–World War I Red Sox, and Joe DiMaggio. The voters decided that Casey Stengel should break the tie, seeing that he had seen both play.

He made his call: "Joe," Stengel said, "did everything so naturally, half the time he gave the impression he

DiMaggio waves his cap to the crowds, Yankee Stadium, 1978. Also, known as Joltin' Joe for his slugging, the graceful but aloof DiMaggio played for the Yankees his entire career from 1936 to 1951, with a 31-month gap while serving in the U. S. Army during World War II. His number 5 is retired and there is a monument (previously a plaque) dedicated to him in Yankee Stadium's Monument Park. He was elected to the National Baseball Hall of Fame in 1955.

Yogi Berra in Pittsburgh for the World Series, 1960. He played for the Yankees from 1946 to 1963, and was later a manager (twice) and a coach for the Yankees. His number 8 (shared with Bill Dickey) is retired and there is a plaque dedicated to him in Monument Park. He was elected to the Baseball Hall of Fame in 1972.

Whitey Ford, 1956. A native New Yorker, Ford played for the Yankees his entire career, from 1950 to 1967. His number 16 is retired and there is a plaque in his honor in Monument Park. He was elected to the Baseball Hall of Fame with Mantle in 1974.

wasn't trying. That is, that's the way it looked to others. On the bench we knew different. It was what some writers call an optical illusion. It was as simple as that—everything he did. He had the greatest instinct of any ballplayer I ever saw. He made the rest of them look like plumbers."

Late in 1950, Joe announced that he would retire after the 1951 season, and he did. In a first-person piece for *Sport*, Joseph Paul DiMaggio described that moment that set him free:

My last time at bat I hit Larry Jansen for a double and was thrown out at third on McDougald's bunt. I got up from the dirt and ran across the field to the Yankee dugout, and all of a sudden the crowd started cheering. Somehow, they guessed they had just seen my last Yankee hit.

The dirt all over him, it was the cry of the aged warrior going out in style, *not with a whimper*. Take a good look at Marvin Newman's emotional 1978 photographs of Joseph Paul DiMaggio at the Yankees' Old Timers' game (see pages 13 and 14). As always, because Joe was who he was, he was the last Yankee to be introduced. There he is, waving his cap at his fans, most of whom had loved him forever. Makes you want to shed a tear, doesn't it?

MICKEY

In January of 1950, the kid from Commerce, Oklahoma, received a letter from Lee MacPhail, director of the Yankees' farm system. A year earlier, in the parked car of a Yankee scout, Tom Greenwade, Mickey Mantle had signed a Class D contract of $140 a month, plus a $1,100 bonus, to become a Yankee. In the letter, MacPhail asked Mickey if, in February, he would like to attend a special one-week school in Phoenix, Arizona, a school for the best minor-league prospects. Mickey was then working as an electrician's helper in Blue Goose No. 1, the same lead and zinc mine as his father, Mutt Mantle. Mickey said he sure would attend the camp.

It was Casey Stengel's idea. Why not a prespring outing just for the Yankees' select baby ballplayers? He was especially interested in the kid he'd heard so much about from the scouts, the kid, he was told, who liked running after jack rabbits back home. (Years later when Mickey had become sort of a down-home storyteller to his Yankee teammates, he told them how he used to chase rabbits back in Commerce. "I'd be fair to them," he said. "I'd chase them in the snow and wouldn't wear spikes or sneakers, and I'd give 'em a fair start.")

Elston Howard, 1955. The first African American to play for the Yankees, he played catcher and in the outfield for the Yankees from 1955 to 1967. After a brief stint with the Boston Red Sox, he then coached for the Yankees from 1969 to 1980.

Roger Maris, 1961, the year he broke Babe Ruth's single-season home run record with 61 home runs. Maris played for the Yankees as an outfielder from 1960 to 1966.

The Yankees treated the school as a big-time operation. Stengel was there with his terrific coaches, Bill Dickey, Frank Crosetti, and Jim Turner; Casey also brought in a faculty made up of the Yankee players he loved on his present squad: Yogi Berra, Tommy Henrich, and Hank Bauer. Casey, of course, was the dean, lecturing the students in the Stengel way. "I like you young fellas," he would say, "I like to play 'em in the big leagues when they're supposed to be too young to play 'em in the big leagues." He had special hopes for Mickey Mantle. He told the eighteen-year-old, "If you ever learn how to bunt from either side with this speed, you ought to hit .400. Now," he waved to him, "you go back out there on the field and keep practicing what they're teaching you."

Well, they were mostly teaching Mantle how to play outfield rather than shortstop. Tommy Henrich hit hundreds of fungoes to the Mick. Hundreds. He also discovered that the kid had a great throwing arm, but needed to learn how to handle a ball from the outfield. As for the kid's hitting, what was there to teach? Bill Dickey, who pitched batting practice to Mickey, told Tom Meany, a well-connected sportswriter of the time (he was Joe DiMaggio's favorite ghost writer), "The boy hit the first

six balls nearly 500 feet, over the lights and out of sight. He hit them over the fence right-handed and he hit them over the fence left-handed."

Mickey spent the 1950 season in Joplin, Missouri, in the Class C Western Association. He did more than okay for the team, batting .383, with 199 hits, 15 of them bunts, and hitting 26 home runs—14 right-handed, 12 left-handed. Joplin won the pennant. Mick had earned his $250 a month salary.

In the spring of 1951, Stengel had another instructional camp for his favored youngsters. He was happy to see how Mickey had filled out. He was not a six-footer; they put him down at 5'11," and maybe that was a bit of an exaggeration. But he weighed 180 muscular pounds, with a seventeen-inch neck, extra powerful arms, back and leg muscles. Dashing around the base paths with his head down and arms pumping, he looked like a world-class sprinter who has just exploded out of the starting block.

When this baby camp broke up Stengel asked three of his hopefuls to stay on for spring training: a twenty-three-year-old third baseman, Gil McDougald; a twenty-one-year-old pitcher, Tom Morgan; and the nineteen-year-old Mickey Mantle. They all made it to the varsity team in 1951.

Opening day, and Mickey Mantle would be in the starting lineup, batting third; DiMaggio the clean-up hitter; Yogi Berra batting fifth. Mantle deserved to be in there after batting .402 through spring training. But almost immediately, he found himself having a tough time all around. Leaping from Class C to the biggies all at once, he had trouble catching on to major-league pitching. And despite all the help he had gotten from Henrich, turning him into an outfielder, he was hardly a "natural" out there.

Above everything else, this shy youngster from the sticks suddenly found himself under intense pressure in the outside world. Jack Orr, a fine columnist for the *New York Compass* put it this way: "He is disturbed by the mail and the girls and the kids and the subway rides. He has a feeling that he's being pushed around."

On July 15, batting .260, having struck out 52 times in 69 games, he was sent to Kansas City.

Mutt Mantle decided to make an emergency visit to his son. He found the boy completely down on himself. "I'm just not cut out for baseball," he wailed to his father. "Maybe I ought to quit."

"If that's all the guts you got," Mutt said, "pack up and come home with me and be a miner." The son was shocked by his father's words, and there was a sudden silence between them. "You can't have it easy all your life," Mutt went on. "Baseball is no different from any other job. Things get tough once in awhile and you must learn how to take it—and the sooner, the better."

It came sooner for Mickey. He went on to play 40 games for Kansas City. He batted .361, drove in 50 runs, and hit 11 homers. On August 8, he came back to the Yankees. In the last 37 games of the season, Mickey's batting average rose to .283. And he helped the Yankees win the pennant by five games over Cleveland.

It had been a learning year for him: learning how to become a great outfielder, not just a good one; learning how to go after major-league pitchers; learning better how to deal with himself off the field, though he would never master that art. He couldn't wait to play in the World Series against those miracle New York Giants who had just beaten the Dodgers, thanks to Bobby Thomson's last-second home run, a shot that came to be mythologized—may I say?—round the world. In Game 1, Mickey would lead off and play right field.

I had been at *Sport* magazine for eight months, loving every minute of it, when my boss, Ed Fitzgerald, gave me a press pass for the second game of the World Series. It would be the second World Series game I'd seen *live*. The other one was in 1948, the first game of the series between the Cleveland Indians and my team, the Boston Braves. My uncle Arky, a great man who had helped install the lights at Braves Field, got me a job as an usher. I don't remember doing much ushering that afternoon. I was

Mickey Mantle, 1956. Mantle played for the Yankees from 1951 to 1968. His number 7 is retired and a monument was built (previously a plaque) to honor him in Monument Park.

mostly watching Bob Feller against Johnny Sain; a terrific pitching duel won by my Braves, 1–0.

I may be exaggerating because I was also a rookie in '51, but I felt so lucky to be starting out during one of the most marvelous baseball seasons ever, especially if you were a New Yorker, which I now was. It was New York baseball that prevailed. Here were the Giants, in the World Series after their amazing last-minute run at the Dodgers, punctuated by the Bobby Thomson home run. Here was the great Dodger catcher, Roy Campanella, winning the Most Valuable Player award in the National League. Here was the great Yankee catcher, Yogi Berra, winning the Most Valuable Player award in the American League. Here, too, was a superb pitching staff. Both Vic Raschi and Ed Lopat won 21 games. How could Allie Reynolds match their performances? Well, Allie did pitch *two* no-hitters in that one season. The pitching would have been even deeper if Whitey Ford had been with them. Twenty-two years old in 1950, Whitey showed what he had, going 9–1. But with the Korean War raging he served in the army for the next two years.

At the beginning of the season, the rookie, Mickey Mantle was generating the loudest noise. But he didn't win the 1951 Rookie of the Year award. That honor went to his teammate, Gil McDougald. And in the other league

Casey Stengel, also known as "The Old Perfesser," c. 1956. Stengel played in the major leagues in Brooklyn, Pittsburgh, Philadelphia, New York, and Boston. He began working his way through the same cities as a manager, with the Brooklyn Dodgers and the Boston Braves, before coming to New York where he at last met with success. He skippered the Yankees to seven World Series titles and ten American League pennants. His number 37 is retired and a plaque is dedicated to him in Monument Park. He was elected to the Baseball Hall of Fame in 1966.

who should win it but the rookie who made the loudest noise for most of the season: Willie Mays. And in the first inning of the first World Series game, it was Willie's roommate, Monte Irvin, showing the way for the Giants by stealing home. The Cinderella Giants went on to win the opener, 5–1.

The press pass I was carrying to the stadium for Game 2 put me in the auxiliary press box. The regular press box, overlooking home plate, could never accommodate all the sportswriters from all over the United States. The auxiliary press box, with the longest picnic table you've ever seen, was for the working stiffs to put their typewriters, notebooks, binoculars, or hot dogs on. It began where the regular press box ended, on the mezzanine level down past third base well into left field. It was all right for me. I would sit anywhere in this ballpark for this game on this day.

My seat had good sighting of the outfield, especially from center field to right field. It offered me a close-up to

The Great Convergence of Game 2, involving three players whose names would never be forgotten in the history of the national pastime: Joe DiMaggio, Willie Mays, and Mickey Mantle.

It was the top of the fifth inning, the Yankees leading 2–1 in a tight pitching duel between Ed Lopat and the Giants' ace, Larry Jansen. The batter was Willie Mays and he lofted a fly ball to right center. DiMaggio started for the ball. So did Mantle, who was shaded towards right center. He had been told more than once that when DiMaggio was going after a ball, to let him be. He heard his teammate call for it. At the same time—as though he'd been shot—Mickey fell to the ground. Later, Mickey said the sound was like a tire blowing out. DiMaggio caught the ball and then looked down at Mantle. He saw that the kid's eyes were closed. He didn't know what had happened. Later DiMaggio told a writer, "At first I thought he was dead." But when Mantle opened his eyes he burst out crying and DiMaggio leaned over and said, "Don't move. They're bringing a stretcher."

When Mickey came back to life, he told those around him, "I think the spikes of my right shoe caught the rubber cover of a sprinkler head buried in the grass." All he knew now was that his right knee had collapsed.

Mutt Mantle, who was sitting close to the dugout, was in the trainer's room when they brought in his son. The Yankee doctor put splints on both sides of Mickey's leg. They gave Mickey crutches and he and his father were driven back to their hotel.

The next morning they took a cab to Lenox Hill Hospital. Mutt got out of the taxi, but Mickey, with his crutches, had a difficult time pulling himself out of the car. Mutt was standing, waiting for Mickey. Needing to steady himself, Mickey reached out for his father's shoulder and Mutt Mantle fell to the sidewalk.

They were both rushed into the hospital. They put Mutt in bed; he and his son would room together. Mickey went to the operating room where an orthopedic surgeon repaired two torn ligaments in Mickey's right knee.

Father and son watched the rest of the World Series, which the Yankees won in six games. Doctors had given Mutt Mantle a series of tests. The news was bad. He was diagnosed with Hodgkin's disease, a cancer that had killed Mantle's grandfather and uncle. After the series, Mutt went back home to Oklahoma. Mantle stayed in New York for rehabilitation, not knowing what the future held for him.

Casey Stengel, the man who thought that Mickey could bat .400 by just beating out bunts, was staggered by the event. That blinding speed was gone, he was sure. What would the kid have left?

Coming in for spring training in 1952 it was plain to Mickey that his leg had not fully healed. Mickey didn't get into a game until mid-March. And then Stengel put him into right field. On May 6, Mantle received somber news, though he knew it was coming. Mutt Mantle had died. After the funeral and a short stay with his family, Mickey came back to the Yankees. He never felt so down in his life. He'd lost his father, he didn't know where he would be playing, but he did know that he would always play in pain. On May 20, Stengel put him into center field.

Before every game, Mickey sat by his locker wrapping both legs from thigh to ankle, in tight, rubberized bandages. (See page 48.) Once, he submitted to a locker-room interview with broadcaster Howard Cosell, who looked at

just got to worry about whether it's ever going to stop hurting. That's the only thing I ever worry about."

And then he went on a spree. On July 13, for the first time, Mickey hit a home run left-handed and a home run right-handed. In the midst of what seemed to be the kid's renewal, a reporter asked the manager if it was real. "Sure," Casey Stengel said, "I think Mantle is the most improved player in the league. Why shouldn't I? Ever since we put the kid in center regularly, we've been winning regularly, haven't we?"

the bandaging and asked Mickey, "Do you have to do that every day?"

"I think I could maybe do without it," Mickey said, "but along about the fifth or sixth inning the leg would start to get tired."

Cosell, who built a formidable broadcasting career by asking tough questions, asked Mickey, "Do you worry about the leg curtailing your career?"

"The only thing that worries me," Mickey said, "is that after a doubleheader I come home and it hurts, and you

They had. On September 26, the Yanks clinched their fourth straight pennant.

YOGI

I don't think there's anything better a man could say about his life than there's nothing else he would rather be than what he is. If you can say that and mean it, you've got it made. Don't get me wrong. I'm not bragging that being Yogi Berra is better than being anybody else in the world. I don't mean that at all. What I mean is I've been blessed with being the only thing I ever wanted to be, a ballplayer, and I wouldn't trade places with anybody.

That's what Yogi Berra told the world in *Sport* magazine when he was at his best, a key ballplayer for the New York Yankees in the time of their dynasty. All right, Yogi never talked that way. He had help from a ghostwriter, but the sentiments were truly his. In a 1962 book , *The October Twelve*, about the Yankees' super year of 1961, Phil Rizzuto said, "I would say that Yogi has been the most valuable Yankee over the past

ing there in uniform, trimmer than most of the other old-timers, ready to play, smiling to the world in the *New York Times*.

Yet the Yankees almost lost him in the middle of his heroic years. Mickey Mantle, with the help of sportswriter Jack Zanger, wrote a lovely piece about Yogi in *Sport*. It was called "The Yogi Berra I Know." In it was a revelatory story about Yogi's fight with the front office in 1954.

"I know," Mickey said, "Yogi is once supposed to have said, 'How do you expect me to think and hit at the same

fifteen years. Without him, the Yankees couldn't have accomplished what they did."

I couldn't help thinking of Yogi as I watched the festivities at the Old Timers' game in August of 2008. The Yankees outdid themselves by inviting 72 old-timers for a last hurrah at the old stadium. It was great seeing Whitey Ford, Reggie Jackson, Don Larsen, Wade Boggs, Tino Martinez, the Yankees' newest Hall of Famer, Goose Gossage, and all the others. The last one to be introduced (with Joe DiMaggio and Mickey Mantle gone) was Yogi Berra. There he was, all by himself, a palace guard, stand-

A powerful switch-hitter, here Mickey Mantle batting right-handed.

time?' I'd rather point to the time he was having a salary dispute with George Weiss after the 1954 season. A lot of people were saying that Yogi would win the Most Valuable Player award. But Mr. Weiss told him some of the other papers favored other players and that it wasn't official yet. And Yogi said, 'I only read the papers which say I'm the most valuable.'" Well, he did win the MVP in 1954 as he did in 1951, and would a third time in 1955. And he got close to what he wanted.

Elio Chacón called safe at the plate; Elston Howard catching, 1961 World Series, Yankees vs. Cincinnati Reds.

YOGI AND MICKEY

Casey Stengel came to rely the most on two Yankees during his reign, and thus came to love them: they were Berra and Mantle. Casey knew—he saw it every day, both men playing all-out—Mantle never without pain, Berra never with a rest. In his Berra piece for *Sport*, Mickey mentions how often, in Stengel's presence, Yogi complained about aches and pains. "But Casey knew how to handle him," Mickey said. "Yogi'd stare at him with those sad eyes," Mickey wrote, "and tell Casey he had a bruised finger, and ol' Case would keep looking down and filling out his lineup card and say, 'I'm too busy now. Talk to me about it after the ball game.'"

Berra did once give his side of the story. "The one thing I said to people when they asked me was it true that Casey Stengel liked me as much as the newspapers were always writing he did. I told them, he must have because he sure played me. As Casey is always saying, you could look it up." I did. Yogi caught over 100 games a season for fourteen years in a row. In two years, 1950 and 1954, Yogi caught in 151 games. All told he was the Yankee catcher for 2,120 games.

He was certainly the guy in the Yankees' glory years who kept it going. In 1952, when the Yankees clinched their fourth straight pennant, Berra hit 30 home runs, and drove in 98. In the seven-game World Series with the Brooklyn Dodgers, his two home runs helped the Yankees win their fourth straight world championship.

In 1953, when the Yankees coasted in, beating Cleveland by 8 ½ games, Berra hit 27 home runs, drove in 108, and had the third best slugging average in the league. In the World Series, again against their mortal enemies, the Dodgers, who had won 105 games, Berra batted .429. He still holds World Series' records for games by a catcher (63), hits (71), and times played on the winning team (10). Mickey Mantle, who had grown up by then, always said about Yogi's hitting that "I've still yet to see anybody get a fastball by him," and concluded by saying, "He's got the quickest wrists I ever saw. I'd give anything to have wrists like Yogi's." On defense, Yogi led American League catchers in assists and fielding—three times each. He was a 15-time All-Star.

And so under Casey Stengel the Yankees set a record that has yet to be equaled: winning five pennants and five world championships in a row. Of course, it had to end sometime. It did in 1954. The Yankees won 103 games that season, but the Cleveland Indians finally broke through by winning 111 games. Blame it the most on the Indians' savage pitchers, who were at their peak. Early Wynn and Bob Lemon both won 23 games, and Mike Garcia won 19 and led all pitchers with a 2.64 earned run average.

After Cleveland clinched the pennant, Casey let up on his troops somewhat. In a September 26 game against Philadelphia, the Yankees lost 8–6, perhaps because he let

Yogi Berra play third base and Mickey Mantle play shortstop. Stengel called it his "power line up." It didn't work.

In 1955, the Yankees got serious again.

WHITEY

In his magical 16-year romp with the Yankees, Ed "Whitey" Ford was a 20-game winner only twice. That bothered some of his teammates, but it never bothered Ford, or his manager, Casey Stengel. "If you had one game to win," said Casey Stengel, "and your life depended on it, you'd want him to pitch it." Especially in the World Series. Ford was the one who broke Babe Ruth's forty-five-year-old record of 29 2/3 scoreless innings in World Series competition.

He was that rare figure on the Yankees, born and raised on the streets of New York. In 1947, Ford signed a Yankee contract right out of high school. Three years later, in July of 1950, he was called up by Stengel to pitch a game against the Detroit Tigers in Detroit. The Tigers were pesky that year, chasing the Yankees for the pennant, ending up just three games behind. And in that first major-league game of his life, the rookie showed them something. Helped by a DiMaggio home run in the sixth inning, Eddie Ford held the Tigers hitless over seven innings. In the eighth, though, the Tigers tied the game with back-to-back doubles. The Rook was the first batter in the ninth. Casey must have had a hunch or something. He refused to call on a pinch hitter. Ford managed a walk. And then the Yankees scored 7 runs, and the youngster had his first major-league win. The next morning he saw a New York newspaper that had this headline: *Ford, DiMaggio Beat Tigers*. He ended up buying 49 more and mailing them home.

Of his nine wins in 1950 (against one loss) the rookie also pitched the fourth game of the World Series against Philadelphia. Yogi Berra hit a home run in the first, and Ford felt so good about it, he held the Phillies scoreless through the eighth inning. In the ninth he slowed up and the Phillies scored 2 runs, but Allie Reynolds came in and struck out the final batter.

People were impressed by Ford's toughness. Richard Ben Cramer, in his book on Joe DiMaggio, wrote that the rookie Ford was "just a runt" who "had plenty of guts, and brought to the mound all the moxie of the New York streets where he'd learned to play."

Whitey, still in the army, came home on leave one weekend in '51 to get married. Casey Stengel insisted that the entire team attend. A bus carrying the Yankees showed up for the reception at Donahue's Bar in Astoria, Queens. All but one of the players had a hearty time. Mickey Mantle, an absurdly shy newcomer who had never met Ford, stayed on the bus. Later that evening Whitey and his wife, Joan, accompanied the players back to the bus. There they were both introduced to the reticent Mantle. "I remember my impression of him the

Yankee second baseman Bobby Richardson throwing and San Francisco Giant Orlando Cepeda sliding in a double play, 1962 World Series, Yankees vs. Giants.

first time I met him," Whitey said later. "What a hayseed." Over the years Mickey and Whitey became best friends. In 1974 they were both inducted into the Hall of Fame.

Ford came back in 1953, cheered by all his friends, including Mantle, and he won 18 games. In 1954, the year that the Yankees did not win the pennant, Ford went 16–6.

In 1955, helped mightily by Ford, who led the league with 18 wins and an incredible 18 complete games, the Yankees recovered their charm, winning the pennant by three games over—who else?—Cleveland. There, too, was Mickey Mantle leading the league with 37 home runs. In the heartbreaking seven-game World Series against the Dodgers, Whitey was touched up for 4 runs in Game 1, but won it 6–5. In the sixth game he beat the Dodgers 5–1. But in Game 7, the decider, Johnny Podres pitched the game of his life, a 2–0 shutout of the Yankees, making Brooklyn the world champions.

Whitey often liked to philosophize about his success. Once he was heard to say, "It was righteous living, you

know. Don't drink everything in the bottle. Leave some for the other guy."

ELSTON

There was also an historic moment for the Yankees in 1955. Elston Howard became the first African American to wear a Yankee uniform.

With the National League way ahead of the American League in finding black ballplayers, the pressure was on the Yankees (who were after all the greatest team of them all in those years) to break their obvious color line. They looked carefully for the person who would be fit to wear Yankee pinstripes. In 1950, they found the one they wanted. Elston Howard was a perfect choice. His parents were of the educated middle class. His father was a high school principal in the St. Louis area. His mother wanted Elston to become a doctor. And Casey Stengel wanted him to fill out his platoon as a catcher and outfielder. Howard was then playing for one of the finest Negro teams, the Kansas City Monarchs. The Yankees gave the Monarchs $30,000 for the serious six-foot-two, 210-pound prospect.

Soon after his signing, Howard was swept into the army for two years. He came back in 1953, and in 1954, playing for Toronto in the International League, he batted .330 and won the league's Most Valuable Player award. Stengel brought him up in 1955.

And Elston was an immediate help. He played 75 of his 95 games in the outfield, the others as catcher and sometime first baseman, and he batted .290. In Game 1 of the 1955 World Series, the game won by Whitey Ford, Elston contributed a two-run home run.

In 1956, when the Yankees righted themselves in the World Series against public enemy No. 1, the Dodgers, Howard hit a home run in the seventh and deciding game, won by the Yankees 9–0. It should be noted that Yogi helped, too. He also hit a home run in that seventh game. All in all in the series, he batted .360 with 3 home runs and 10 runs batted in. Of course, he will ever be remembered, not for his hitting, but for the leap and loving hug of his life on a baseball diamond (captured by Marvin Newman on page 84).

DON

It is time to talk about Don Larsen. A strapping six-foot-four, 225 pounder, Larsen liked to mope around during the day; he came truly alive only at night. Casey Stengel once said of him, "The only thing he fears is sleep." But Casey liked that kind of a person and he gave Larsen the job of pitching Game 2 against the Dodgers. Having lost the first game to the Dodgers 6–3, the Yankees needed a performance from the "Nightrider," as his teammates called him. Those teammates did well for Don, giving him 1 run in the first and 5 more in the second. With the bases loaded, Yogi hit a home run in the top of the second which served as the centerpiece of that rally.

But it turned out it was not good enough. In the last of the second inning the Dodgers scored their 6 runs. And Stengel walked out to the mound and said to Larsen, "Enough for today." Donald went off muttering to himself, "That's the last time I'll ever go to bed early." The Dodgers won it 13–8.

Then the Yankees came back, winning the third and fourth games to even the series. And Casey announced that Larsen would pitch the fifth game. That night Larsen went out with a sportswriter friend, and they drank some beer as the night wore on. Larsen took a slice of pizza to bed with him at 1 A.M. Then off to sleep; he had a job to do tomorrow.

How lucky for me. My boss at *Sport,* Ed Fitzgerald, gave me a ticket for the game. Marvin Newman would also attend the game. He was there on assignment from *Look* magazine to photograph the Dodgers' starting pitcher, Sal Maglie. One tends to forget that Maglie pitched the whole game too, and allowed the Yankees only 5 hits, one a Mickey Mantle blast in the fourth inning. Mickey also made the defensive play of the game in the fifth inning. Gil Hodges, the Dodgers' peerless first baseman, hit a low line drive that headed out to deep left-center field toward the fence. Mickey raced to his right and back, running diagonally. At the last split second he reached high, trying to backhand the ball. The ball caught in his glove and he squeezed it, breaking his stride as he hit the warning track deep in the outfield.

As you will see, Marvin also caught that catch with his camera as he began to disobey *Look,* switching from Maglie to Larsen when he understood what was going on—a possible no-hitter in the making.

By the ninth inning, Marvin was shooting everything on the field that moved, including the called third strike on pinch-hitter Dale Mitchell that closed out the game. And—look!—there was Yogi out on the mound, jumping onto Larsen's body, locking his legs around the hero of heroes, squeezing the pitcher to death.

It was Shirley Povich of the *Washington Post,* who wrote the prize-winning story of Larsen's perfect game. Here is his lead: "The million-to-one-shot came in. Hell froze over. A month of Sundays hit the calendar. Don Larsen today pitched a no-hit, no-run, no-man-reach-first game in a World Series."

WHITEY AND WARREN

What could the next two World Series, between the Milwaukee Braves and the Yankees, provide? Well, probably not another perfect game, although the Braves in particular did have strong pitching, led by Warren Spahn, who won 21 games in 1957, while his pitching mate, Lew Burdette, won 17. The Braves had a brutal lineup of sluggers, with third baseman Ed Mathews, first baseman Joe Adcock, outfielder Bill Bruton, and the greatest hitter of them all, Hank Aaron. In '57, Aaron won the pennant for the Braves with his eleventh inning home run against the runner-up, the St. Louis Cardinals. And he led the league in home runs with 44; runs batted in, 132; runs scored, 118.

The Yankees had won the pennant, thanks mostly to Mickey Mantle. He was first in the league in runs scored, 121; first on bases on balls, 146; second in batting average to Ted Williams. 365; and third in home runs, 34; He even finished fourth in stolen bases with 16 out of 18. And he won his second MVP. Yet, the Yankees were absolutely stymied by the tremendous pitching of Milwaukee's Lew Burdette. In Game 1, there was a perfect pitching duel between two of baseball's greatest left-handed pitchers: Whitey Ford vs. Warren Spahn. It was Ford winning, 4–3. But Burdette was the Braves' iron man. He won Game 2. He won Game 5, a brilliant 1–0 shutout against Whitey Ford. And with only two days of rest in Game 7, he shut out the Yankees again, 6–0.

It was a series that seriously unraveled Casey Stengel, especially the way Burdette handled his men. "It's the first time since I managed that I had a man who

Warren Spahn on the mound for the Milwaukee Braves. The Yankees played the Milwaukee Braves in the World Series in 1957 and 1958.

disturbed a ball club like he disturbed us. He had every batter the same way, sort of confused. We couldn't get a solid hit off him."

And then as the 1958 World Series came along, he was angry by what Lew Burdette said to the press, that the Yankees would not be a winning team in the National League. His embarrassment was magnified when the Braves took a 3–1 lead against the Yankees.

Game 1 was almost an exact replica of the first game in 1957 except that this time Spahn beat Ford, 4–3. And then, with Burdette pitching, the Braves won Game 2, 13–5. Burdette even hit a home run in that one. Mickey Mantle, however, topped Burdette at bat, hitting 2 home runs. In Game 3, Don Larsen (bless him for staying up late) pitched a 4–0 shutout. And then came Spahn and Ford in Game 4. This time Spahn pitched a brilliant 2–0, two-hit shutout.

So the Braves needed only one game to win, to make it two world championships in a row. But Yankee Bob Turley, a young pitcher growing up fast, shut out Milwaukee, 7–0. Game 6 was the third match-up between Ford and Spahn. Whitey lasted but one inning. Spahn pitched the entire game that went into the tenth inning. Gil McDougald hit a home run in the top of the tenth, and

Bill Skowron singled home a second run. Casey called on Bob Turley to pitch to the last Brave standing. He made the save. New York, 4–3.

The grand finale featured Don Larsen vs. Lew Burdette. Casey Stengel took out Larsen in the third even though the score was 2–1 Yankees, and inserted his man, Turley. (Turley had won 21 games for the Yankees in '58 and pitched 22 complete games, winning the American League's Cy Young Award for his efforts.) In the sixth, Milwaukee catcher Del Crandall hit a home run to tie the game at 2–2. But in the top of the eighth, Bill Skowron hit a three-run home run off of Burdette. The Yankees won 6–2, they won it all.

Right after the game in the dressing room, Casey Stengel got on the podium and said to the crowd of reporters, "Maybe now that fella over there will think we're good enough to play in the other league."

The Yankees were world champions again—Casey Stengel's seventh world championship.

The next two years were not the best in the Stengel saga. In 1959, the Yankees failed to win anything. In fact, they finished third in the league, 15 games behind the Chicago White Sox, who won their first pennant in forty years (but would then lose to the Los Angeles Dodgers). On May 11 at Yankee Stadium, Yogi Berra made his first error in 148 games. After the season, a half-dozen of the best Yankees had to take pay cuts.

In 1960, the turnaround was amazing. It was the year that Mantle was at his best. It was the year that Roger Maris was at his best. It was the year of Casey Stengel, too, who turned seventy and received a proper public birthday party. And it was the year when second baseman Bill Mazeroski came to the plate in the last of the ninth inning with the game tied, 9–9.

It was a tremendous World Series, full of high-scoring games. The Yankees won one 16–3, another 12–0. Through six games and eight and a half innings of the seventh game, the Yankees had outscored the Pirates by 29 runs. And then came the deciding game. There were 4 home runs struck—by Rocky Nelson and catcher Hal Smith of the Pirates, and Yogi Berra and Bill Skowron of the Yankees. Forget them all. It was 9–9 in the bottom of the ninth, and Bill Mazeroski was at the plate.

Throughout the game Marvin Newman was hanging in the stands behind home plate, with the medium telephoto lens he had on his camera. He wanted to get the shot that would be the most significant moment of the game. What he saw, he explained in a marvelous HBO documentary about the game, "was that you could photograph through home plate, with the batter and scoreboard together in one picture. I kept going back to this one place in the stands behind home plate." He kept going back there, because he felt that was the place to be if something special happened. And he had a feeling in his bones.

Now look at the photograph (page 120), shot indeed from Marvin's turf. Everything is in it: Mazeroski, No. 9, is in his after-swing. The ball, sailing towards the fence, is there for you to see. Right fielder Yogi Berra watches the flight of the ball; there would be no one for him to hug. And the clock on top of the scoreboard deep in center field can be read, the clock that freezes forever at 3:35 P.M.

Mazeroski prevailed. The Yankees were out of it.

The Yankee owners were pissed by the finish. They had been in talks about selling their team to CBS. A World Series victory would have been nice. And so changes would have to be made.

As soon as the season was over, the owners retired the general manager, George Weiss. And they retired the man who had given them 10 pennants and 7 world championships in his 12 years on the job. On July 30, 1960, they had feted Casey Stengel on his seventieth birthday. Now he was gone. Casey's response was crisp: "I'll never make the mistake of being seventy again."

MICKEY AND ROGER

The World Series outcome may have bruised New York Yankee executives, but both Mickey Mantle and Roger Maris had had sensational seasons.

Mantle led the league in runs scored with 119; Maris was second with 96. Mantle hit 40 home runs; Maris 39. Mantle had 294 total bases; Maris 290. Maris led the league in runs batted in with 112. In the Most Valuable Player voting, Maris got three more votes than Mantle. In the hot summer of 1961, the teammates decided to room together.

Actually, it was Yankee outfielder Bob Cerv who brought them together. In a *Sport* magazine story titled, "My Roommates Maris and Mantle," Cerv (with help from sportswriter Til Ferdenzi) told how it had all come about.

Maris had just hit his fiftieth home run, and he wanted to show his roomie, Cerv, his forearms. "Roger's arms, in fact his whole body," Cerv wrote, "were completely covered with goose bumps. Every time Roger hit one into the seats, he'd break out in goose bumps."

When the surreal 1961 season began, Roger and Cerv were sharing a room in the Hotel Manhattan. "But too many people knew where we lived and the phone rang all the time," Cerv said, "especially after Rog began to slug the ball in the early part of June. One night after a lot of phone calls, Rog turned to me and said, 'Let's look for an apartment.'"

They found a small apartment, far from Manhattan, in the Richmond Hill section of Queens. When Mantle heard about it he asked if he could move in with them. So for $250 a month rent, the two rivals—each out to

Whitey Ford winding up, 1963 World Series, Yankees vs. Los Angeles Dodgers.

break Babe Ruth's sacrosanct 60 home run record—spent August, September, and October in Queens.

It was quiet in Queens for the ballplayers. Mantle read some, Maris checked the sports pages, the television was on, Cerv simply relaxed. The three lived comfortably together. They each cooked their own breakfast, because each liked it done a different way. Bob Cerv liked his bacon and eggs sunny-side up. Mickey cooked his over easy. Roger would do his a little well done. Baseball talk, especially the battle going on between Maris and Mantle, was verboten.

What an astonishing time it was for the 1961 Yankee club. It was a sound club, a versatile club, a club rich in depth, a club with brilliant individual performances for the welfare of the team. As Red Smith put it in 1961 in one of his *New York Herald Tribune* columns, "Ford was the best starting pitcher in the league, Luis Arroyo the best relief pitcher, Elston Howard the best catcher, Tony Kubek the best shortstop, Cletis Boyer infinitely the best defensive third baseman. Roger Maris and Mickey Mantle are of course immortal. Yogi Berra is rich."

The new manager of the Yankees, Ralph Houk, couldn't have asked for more. Right from the beginning, Houk, a major-league catcher for only 91 games (but a real major during World War II) was sure that the players were happy with him. No one was happier than Mickey Mantle. Early in the spring Houk announced to the press that he expected Mantle to be the leader of the club. "You need a leader," Houk said, "and Mantle always had so much going for him. He's one player all the players like. They look up to him." With Mickey's own fresh desire and Houk's careful handling of him, Mickey did become leader of the Yankees.

On September 20, 1961, Ralph Terry won his fifteenth game of the season against the Baltimore Orioles. Yogi Berra hit his twenty-first home run. Roger Maris hit his fifty-ninth home run. And the Yankees clinched the pennant. They would play the Cincinnati Reds in the World Series.

The Reds had a sound but undermanned team. Frank Robinson was their star. He had batted .323 in the season, hit 37 homers, drove in 124 runs, and would win the National League Most Valuable Player award. Vada Pinson, a gifted young outfielder, batted .343, with a league-leading 208 base hits and 23 stolen bases. The Reds' pitching staff was reliable, but not grand: Joey Jay went 21–10. Jim O'Toole was 19–9. Bob Purkey 16–12. None of them came close to Whitey Ford, who had his best season ever, a 25–4 record. He would pitch the opener, against O'Toole.

He allowed the Reds but 2 hits in his 2–0 victory, (one of the Yankee runs, a home run by Elly Howard). Whitey called his outing the best World Series game he'd ever pitched and "among the five best games I've ever pitched in my life."

In the second game, with two out in the top of the fifth, second baseman Elio Chacón looped a single just in front of center fielder Maris. Eddie Kasko then singled to center and Chacón scurried onto third. On the third pitch to Vada Pinson, the ball broke through catcher Howard, rolling back some twelve feet. And Chacón streaked for home. Howard picked up the ball and fell on top of Chacón. The photo (see page 20) shows Howard lying on Chacón, squashing him like a moth. Hold on! The photo also shows the umpire, his mask in hand, waving Chacón safe. That run turned out to be the winning run in the 6–2 game, the Reds only victory.

The hero of Game 3 was Roger Maris, who had been zero for ten so far in the series. Stepping up to the plate in the ninth inning, Roger hit his sixty-second home run to give the Yankees a 3–2 victory. "I'll go zero for ten anytime," Roger said after the game "if I could be sure I'd hit a game-winning home run the eleventh time."

Whitey Ford shut out the Reds again, 7–0, in Game 7. In the bottom of the third, Whitey broke Babe Ruth's record of consecutive scoreless innings. It became 32 for Ford.

There was a sadness to that game. Mantle was in the starting lineup for the first time in the series. He had

an infected thigh and shouldn't have been playing, but he insisted on it. In the fourth inning, Maris walked and Mantle drove a ball to left field. It would have been an easy double, but he barely made it to first base. He limped off the field, blood running from the abscess in his thigh and soaking through his uniform. Clete Boyer, who saw his wound, said the hole was so big you could see the thigh muscles.

The Yankees cleaned out the Reds in Game 5, 13–5. They were world champions once more.

It was Roger Maris who destroyed Babe Ruth's home run record. And it was Roger Maris who, for the second straight year, won the MVP. This time he beat out Mantle by four votes. But Mickey Mantle gained something he had stopped looking for, something that always meant so much to him. He finally gained the love of baseball fans all over the country.

The great Maris-Mantle duel had something to do with it. As Roger began to challenge Babe Ruth's record, Mickey began to get more and more sympathy from the fans. When Mickey hit his fifty-second home run of the season against the Indians on September 2, the 42,000 fans in the stadium stood and applauded while he rounded the bases.

"Those fans," Mickey marveled. "They've changed. I never heard so much cheering in all my years with the club."

Phil Rizzuto had a more logical conclusion about this change. In the last month of the season, Rizzuto said, "They were applauding him because they had begun to realize the kind of courage Mickey Mantle possessed. He played games where you or I or the normal guy would not have been able to creep out of bed."

The applause grew and grew throughout the rest of his career, and lives on today.

MARVIN

Though the Yankees began to spring leaks in 1962, they managed to hold off Minnesota and take the pennant by five games. They then had to face San Francisco, a winner of the playoff with the Dodgers. Marvin Newman was there, (see page 142), shooting for dear life, taking sparkling portraits of Orlando Cepeda and Willie Mays; also several neat game-action shots focusing on Mays. For the Yankees, there were close-ups of Clete Boyer swinging a bat, and Roger Maris crossing home. A shot of Ralph Terry borne on the shoulders of his teammates, happy that he won it for the Yankees. Willie McCovey, in the last at bat for San Francisco, had screamed a liner that was just caught by Bobby Richardson to end it all. And there in the clubhouse after the win, see Ralph Houk drinking champagne and telling the sportswriters how it was accomplished. It would be the last world championship for the Yankees for fifteen years. One solace, though: Mickey Mantle won the MVP award, which he richly deserved.

Yogi Berra tags out Jim Davenport at home plate during the 1962
World Series, Yankees vs. San Francisco Giants.

They were still winning pennants, though, in both
1963 and 1964. Marvin, at both World Series, says it
was pitching that beat them both years. Oh, yes. Sandy
Koufax showed 'em in '63. The first game brought
together Whitey Ford (24–7) and Sandy Koufax (25–5).
Ford lasted to the fifth. Koufax pitched the whole
game, setting a World Series record with 15 strikeouts.
That year, Koufax would not only be the Cy Young winner, but also the MVP.

The Yankees couldn't win a World Series game in 1963,
but they were hopeful about 1964. They made it close.

The most symbolic game of the series was Game 6,
when Maris homered in the sixth inning followed by a
home run from Mickey Mantle that won it for the Yankees.
But Bob Gibson won two out of the three games he pitched
and set a strikeout record for the series with 31 strikeouts.

In every way, the Yankee dynasty was over. Their rookie
manager, Yogi Berra, was fired, and so were many others
in the Yankees' front office. For CBS now owned the team.

The next time the Yankees got into a World Series was
1976. They lost it in four straight against the Cincinnati
Reds. It would take much time for them to come back to
the way it was in the grand old days of DiMaggio, Mantle,
Berra, Ford, Howard, Maris, and all the other sterling
players wearing pinstripes.

Mickey Mantle, the country boy from Commerce, Oklahoma, showing how it's done back home, driving a tractor on Miller Huggins Field during spring training, St. Petersburg, Florida, 1953.

Spring Training

"Oh What a Beautiful Morning." I feel like batting out that song when I find myself in the grasp of a photographer who knows just what he's doing. As I study Marvin Newman's homespun set of photographs taken in St. Petersburg, Florida, during spring training of 1953, I feel the smell of the fresh spring grass under my feet urging me to come to grips with the sweet spring scene.

One reason for my happiness is that it takes me back to my own spring-training days in the years I was working at *Sport*. Early every March, my wife and I either flew or drove to Sarasota, the town we loved so much. At that time the Red Sox were in Sarasota, as was the Ringling Bros. & Barnum and Bailey Circus where you could always smell the elephants, maybe mixed with honeysuckle. Nearby were the Braves in Bradenton, the Reds in Tampa, the Phillies in Clearwater, the old Washington Senators in Fort Myers, and so on. I'd go to peek at all the franchises, trying to find fodder for baseball stories in *Sport*. I always came away with the feeling that everything about baseball down there was fresh and clean.

Looking at Marvin's photos shot that spring, it felt like a family gathering. There was Perfesser Stengel lecturing to a gaggle of kids who'd played in the Yankee farm system before, hoping to make the big jump to the majors. Why, there's ol' Casey again, seeming to be hectoring Mickey a little—the boy has his head down, looking sad. Maybe he's telling Mantle to use the bunt more as an offensive weapon. Sure enough, there's Mantle trying to bunt a ball, his left leg forward, his right leg back, his arms extended. Don't worry about Mickey. He discovered the art of bunting very early in life from his father, Mutt. It's nice to see Stengel with his excellent coaches—Bill Dickey, Frank Crosetti, Jim Turner—who all played for the Yankees in the Joe McCarthy era and were now prime teachers to these kids. When the fans start coming into the stadium either to watch workouts or a game, the players treat them well. There's one right out of the old *Saturday Evening Post*. A young boy taking a picture of Mickey, who is willingly posing, with his happy family looking on. And Yogi, over there, is signing an autograph. The picture that tells it all for me, except maybe for the one they called Mickey's tractor, shows Whitey and Yogi in the locker room, bare-chested, laughing at something as they go for the coffee. Both sixteen-years-old.

Send me back to Florida.

OPPOSITE: Casey Stengel instructing Mickey Mantle, 1953. Charles Dillon Stengel's nickname "Casey" was derived from the initials of his hometown, Kansas City, but sportswriters dubbed him "The Old Perfesser," for his ability to wax eloquently on any aspect of the theme of baseball.

Stengel (with arm raised) instructing the team. Standing, left to right: Gil McDougald, unidentified, Mickey Mantle, Phil Rizzuto, Hank Bauer (kneeling); seated, left to right: Billy Martin, Yogi Berra, and Irv Noren, 1953.

Casey Stengel with his coaches, Frank Crosetti, Bill Dickey, and Jim Turner. One of the great catchers in baseball, first-base coach Bill Dickey played for the Yankees his entire career, from 1928 to 1946. He still holds the World Series record for the most games played as catcher—38. Dickey served a brief stint as manager for the Yankees and later became a coach. He helped develop Yogi Berra into a great catcher. Dickey's number 8 (which he shares with Berra) is retired, he has a plaque in Monument Park, and he was elected to the Baseball Hall of Fame in 1954. Pitching Coach Jim Turner had played as pitcher for the Yankees during the war years, from 1942 to 1945, and coached for the Yankees from 1949 to 1959 and from 1966 to 1973.

Mantle practicing his bunt. Before his knee injury in the 1951 World Series, Mantle was called the fastest man to first base.

Left to right: Coach Crosetti, Gene Woodling, Yogi Berra, and Mickey Mantle. A two-time All-Star, third-base coach Frank Crosetti played shortstop for the Yankees from 1932 to 1948, and coached for the team until 1968. As player and coach, Crosetti participated in 17 World Series championships.

Elston Howard and Yogi Berra warming up before an exhibition
game at Al Lang Field, St. Petersburg, 1957.

Berra at bat and Woodling on deck, in an exhibition game against the Chicago White Sox at Al Lang Field, 1957.

Berra makes a hit and starts toward first.

TOP: In the Yankee dugout at Al Lang Field, left to right: Don Larsen, unidentified player, Jerry Coleman, Yogi Berra, and Gil McDougald.

BOTTOM: Whitey Ford and Yogi Berra around a coffee urn in the locker room after the game.

BERRA S   THRONEBRY

Yogi Berra in front of his locker after the game.

Mickey Mantle horsing around in the locker room with Billy Martin, waiting for Billy to deliver the pitch, as they play with a wiffle ball on a string, prior to a game, 1956.

Inside the Locker Room

Billy Martin washed ashore to Yankeeland in 1950 and promptly became Joe DiMaggio's valet. A raw rookie wise guy, a hell-raiser who would become the team's valuable second baseman; he would do anything DiMaggio directed him to do. He loved playing the fool to his fellow Italian in the two years he had with the great man. Joe came to call Martin "my fresh little bastard."

But then Joe was gone and Billy had to find someone else. Early in the season of 1952, he was rehabilitating a broken ankle suffered in spring training at the same time that Mickey Mantle was doing the same with the leg he had messed up in the 1951 World Series. Newman's photos clearly capture the Mantle-Martin locker-room game; Martin turned to Mantle for friendship and fun.

Soon they were rooming together, drinking together, and planning ways to unsettle their teammates. "Once," said Phil Rizzuto, who was perhaps more vulnerable than anyone else because of his size, "they hung a dead mouse over the steering wheel of my car. I jumped when I saw that, I tell you." There was also the time one spring when the team was barnstorming through Texas that Martin and Mantle disappeared from the hotel. They showed up while their teammates were having dinner, wearing ten-gallon hats with bullet holes in them. "We had a gun duel," Mickey said, solemnly shaking his head.

Every old-time Yankee fan remembers when the fun went out of Martin's life. On the evening of May 16, 1957, Martin's birthday, his pals—Whitey Ford, Hank Bauer, Mickey Mantle, and their wives—went to the famed Copacabana nightclub for dinner and a floor show. It started out jolly for everybody. But in the course of the evening, one of the Yankee players got into a fight with a stranger who was baiting them. It was believed that it was Hank Bauer, not Martin, who had retaliated. The Yankee front office, tired of Martin's shenanigans, chose to believe that he had once again led Mantle astray. A month later, Billy was traded to Kansas City.

It was a loss to the Yankees. Martin especially shone in the clutch during World Series battles. In 1953, the Yankees beat the Brooklyn Dodgers in six games. Martin won the sixth game with a run-scoring single in the bottom of the ninth. He also set a record with 12 hits in a six-game series.

Twenty years later, in 1977, Billy Martin led the Yankees to their first world championship in fifteen years.

Billy Martin takes a swing and misses Mantle's pitch as the toy ball on
a string slides under Martin's bat.

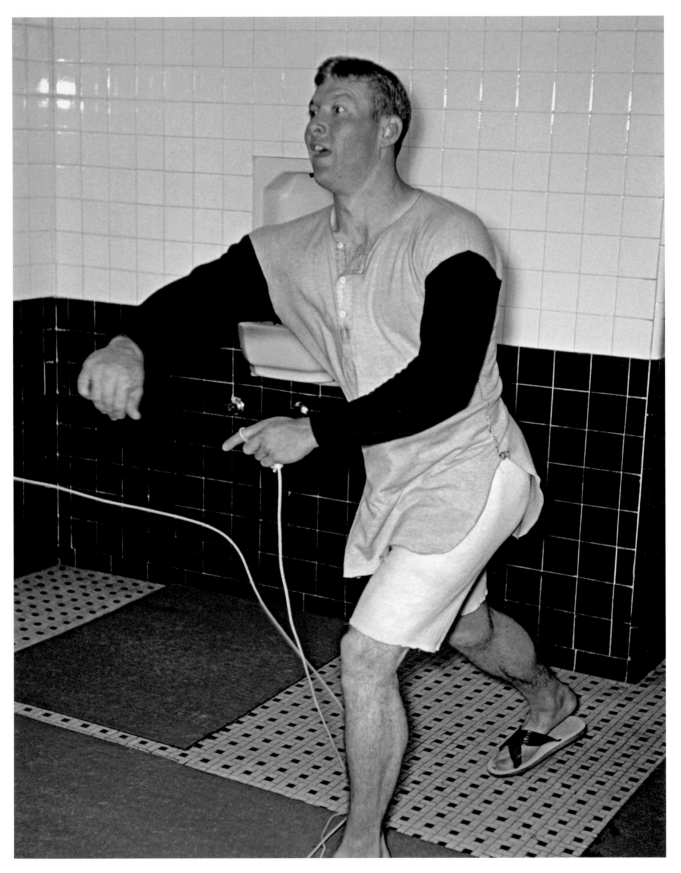

Mickey hurls the toy ball to Billy while holding tight to the
string attachment.

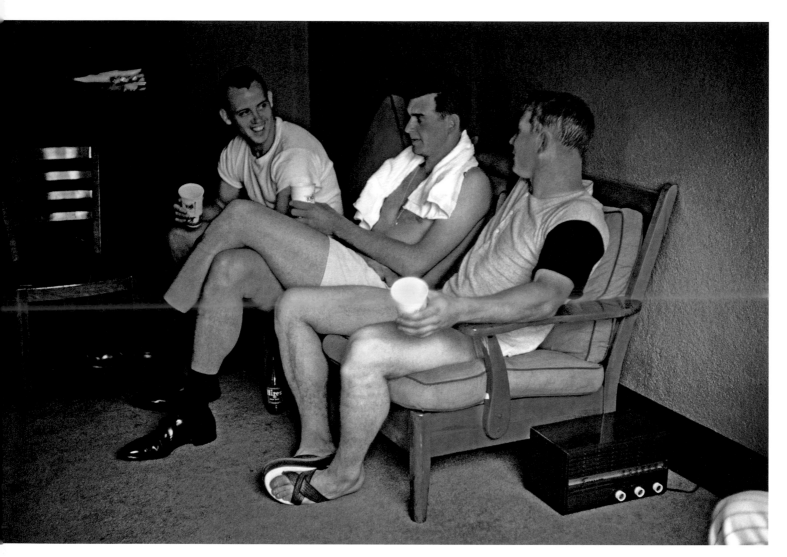

Billy Hunter, a second-string infielder who played for the Yankees from 1955 to 1956, pitcher Don Larsen, and Mickey Mantle winding down with cold drinks after a game, 1955.

OPPOSITE: Billy Martin relaxes after a game, 1955. Martin played second base for the Yankees from 1950 to 1957. He went on to play for six more teams before later becoming a manager. He managed five different major league clubs, including five separate stints managing the Yankees. In his first tenure as Yankee manager, 1975 to 1978, he led the Yankees to two American League pennants. The Yankees were swept by the Cincinnati Reds in the 1977 World Series, but beat the Dodgers in six games in the 1978 World Series. The Yankees retired Martin's number 1 and dedicated a plaque in his honor in Monument Park in 1986.

Before every game, Mantle bandaged both his legs. Mickey's leg
troubles began in high school when he developed osteomyelitis, a
dangerous bone disease, after a football injury went untreated. Later,
in the 1951 World Series against the San Francisco Giants (Mickey's first),
he blew out his right knee when he fell in the outfield. Other knee
injuries had checked his amazing speed, but he still delivered at bat.

Mantle shaving, while another Mickey, left-handed pitcher Mickey McDermott (reflected in the mirror) does the same. McDermott, who played for the Yankees in 1956, was a hot prospect who never lived up to expectations. After playing for six different teams from 1948 to 1961, he ended his career with a win-loss record of 69–69.

Mantle putting on the finishing touches before leaving the
locker room.

Mantle and roommate Billy Martin outside the Hotel Edison in
Manhattan where they lived.

Mantle escapes fans seeking autographs in a car driven by
Berra (unseen) outside the stadium. The talented kid from
Commerce, Oklahoma, came to the big city and became
a star, living up to his newspaper clippings by winning
baseball's Triple Crown, 1956.

Fans fill the bleachers in Yankee Stadium under the illuminated scoreboard, waiting for, hoping to snag a home run ball.

Night Must Fall

In Indianapolis in August of 1930, the Cincinnati Reds played an exhibition game with the Indianapolis Indians—the first night game ever played by a major-league team. But in the early thirties night games were played all over the country by semipro teams and the Negro leagues. It didn't catch on for the major leagues until 1933 when Larry MacPhail was named general manager of the Reds. MacPhail became a zealot for night baseball. In December of 1934, he got the eight National League teams to agree on a maximum of seven games for any teams installing lights. On May 24, 1935, at Crosley Field in Cincinnati, with President Franklin Delano Roosevelt throwing the switch at the White House, the lights went on and the Philadelphia Phillies beat the Reds, 2–1. That year the Reds played one game with each National League team. Attendance averaged 18,000 per game. Playing during the day, the Reds were averaging only 4,700 a game. Night baseball got a real lift on June 15, 1938, when, under the lights, the Reds' Johnny Vander Meer pitched his second successive no-hitter. It came in the first night game ever at Ebbets Field in Brooklyn; the Dodgers had become the second team to install lights. That did it. Maybe some owners felt that there would be more no-hitters if they played at night. They also liked those attendance figures. Night was risen, slowed down only in the World War II years. The Yankees played their first home baseball game under the lights on May 29, 1946, and won.

This portfolio of night baseball photographs matches the majestic sweep and classical facade of Yankee Stadium under the lights. My favorite photo in the group is on page 69, a shot of the front of the stadium with huge red letters on top—YANKEE STADIUM—and underneath, Longines giving "the official time"; the smoky glint on the top of the huge bowl framing the stadium in all its massive glory. It is not only Yankee Stadium itself; but it is also New York bursting with power. Even the hot dog looks like a work of art with a young seller in light clothing, a clean white shirt and white pants offering a customer a dog, all seen more warmly because of the lights (page 59). Another stunning nighttime picture taken on the second tier shows three figures in silhouette looking down on a field that is screaming with light (a Newman specialty is his use of silhouettes). Baseball is truly the national pastime, at night, as well as day.

The twilight hour in the House that Ruth Built. From high in the upper deck along the right field, facing west, under the lattice-like frieze, a majestic view of the interior of the stadium in an early color photograph, 1955. The stadium first opened some thirty-two years earlier on April 18, 1923. It was the first ballpark in the country to be built with a triple deck.

Sharing a joke on the field before the game, left to right: Whitey
Ford, Joe Collins (No. 15), Yogi Berra, Mickey Mantle, and Hank Bauer
at the stadium while the sun still hangs in the west and the stands
have yet to fill with fans.

A hot dog vendor plies his trade down close to the field.

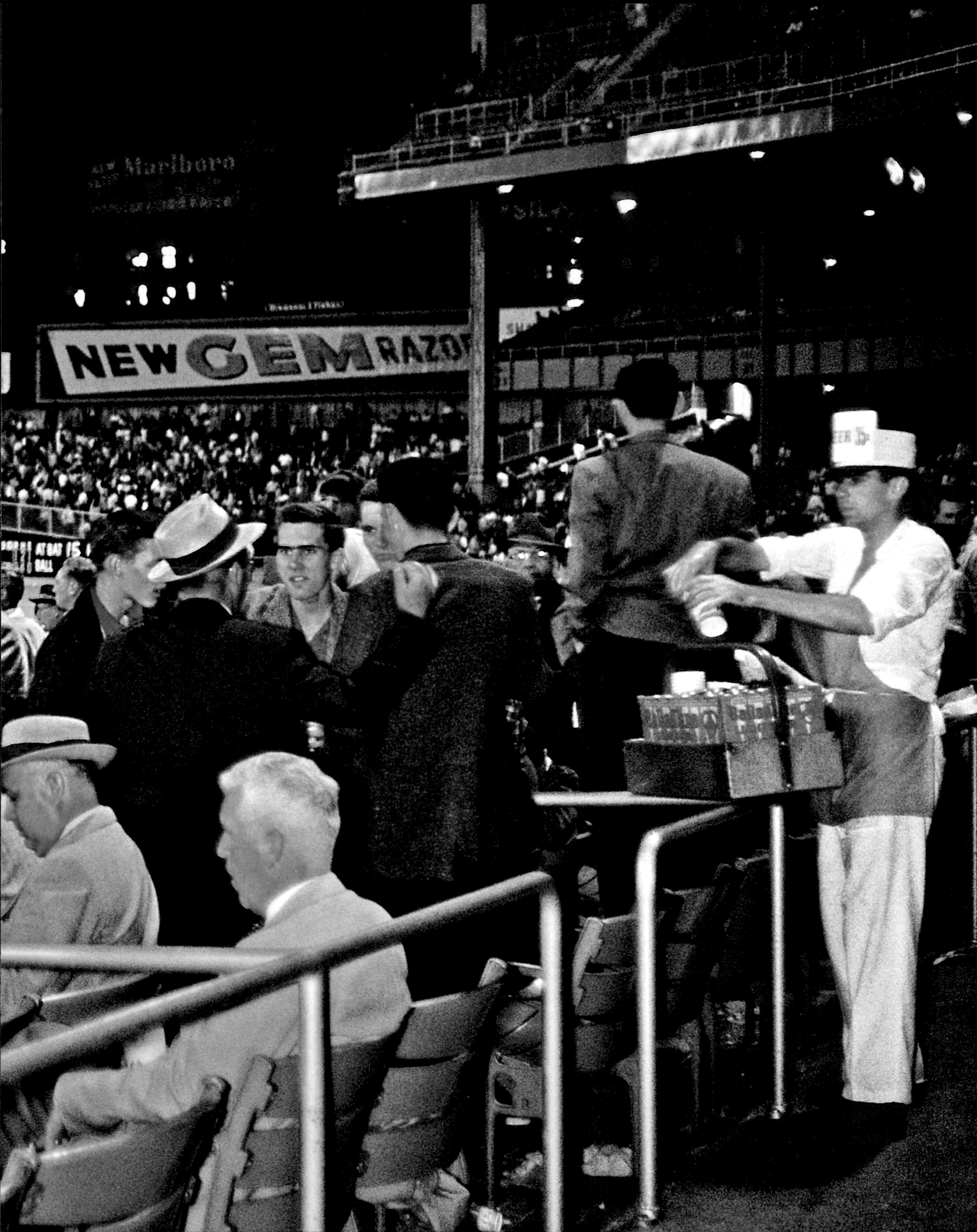
Marlboro
NEW GEM RAZO

Ushers, like sentinels, stand silhouetted against the
illuminated field where a game is in progress.

Viewed from directly above, relief pitchers sit and watch
the game from the bullpen.

Looming up like a great cauldron of baseball magic, Yankee
Stadium at night from outside, the game in progress.
Seeing the glow of the lights, one can imagine the murmur
of the crowd, the signature inflections of Bob Sheppard's
voice over the public-address system, and then suddenly
the roar of the fans, in delight or dismay, at some urgent
development on the field.

Jackie Robinson and Pee Wee Reese at Ebbets Field, 1955. The 1955 World Series was won by the Brooklyn Dodgers, their first championship title, and their only World Series victory in Brooklyn.

1955–1956 World Series vs. Brooklyn Dodgers

The Dodgers and Yankees faced each other for the sixth and seventh time in the last fifteen years, and each series went all the way.

In 1955, the Yankees won the first two games, and the Dodgers won the next three, and you could hardly pull the two teams apart. For the Dodgers, with Jackie Robinson and Pee Wee Reese, Duke Snider, Carl Furillo, Gil Hodges, and Roy Campanella, the pitchers Don Newcombe, Clem Labine, Carl Erskine, and Billy Loes aiming at Campanella's big glove of hope, it was the Boys of Summer at full strength. Casey Stengel never referred to his Yankees as "boys," but there was Yogi Berra with 10 hits and Billy Martin with 8 hits and 4 runs batted in. (Mickey Mantle could only play in three games because of a leg injury.) And yet the heroes of the last two games were not page 3 celebrities. In the sixth game, first baseman Bill Skowron hit a three-run homer in the first inning. That made it easy for Whitey Ford. In the seventh game, a part-time Dodger outfielder, Sandy Amoros, made the play of the series. It saved pitcher Johnny Podres's life. It was the last of the sixth, the Dodgers behind Podres, leading the Yankees 2–0, when Amoros came in to play left field. Yogi Berra was up with a runner at second base. And he hit a bullet towards left field. Amoros raced for the ball over to the wall, stretched his gloved arm out as far as he could, and made a breathtaking one-handed catch. He then fired the ball to Pee Wee Reese who sped it to first baseman Gil Hodges for the double play. The game ended 2–0. It was the Dodgers first World Championship in fifty-five years.

There's been a lot of talk about Don Larsen and his contribution to the history of baseball. The 1956 World Series was, of course, the Don Larsen series. But, look, it was only one of seven games. It was a series between the two teams much like the year before. Only this time the Dodgers, not the Yankees, won the first two games, and the Yankees won the next three, the fifth being the Don Larsen extravaganza. In Game 6, Clem Labine was Larsen personified. Labine allowed the Yankees no runs for nine innings, but Bob Turley also allowed no runs for nine innings. And then, in the last of the tenth, with two out, Jackie Robinson offered the Dodgers a seventh game. He sent a line drive over the left fielder's head, allowing Jim Gilliam, who had been on second base, to streak in with the only run of the game. Game 7. What do you know? It was the third straight shutout of the series—a 9–0 victory for the Yankees' Johnny Kucks over Don Newcombe. It was highlighted by 2 home runs from Berra (he also batted .360 in the series, with 10 RBIs) and one each from Elston Howard and Bill Skowron. The Yankees had not only avenged their 1955 loss, but also won their sixth World Championships in eight years.

Pee Wee Reese, Gil Hodges, Duke Snider, and Jackie Robinson—the legendary Boys of Summer—before the big game, 1955. Reese, Snider, and Robinson were elected to the Hall of Fame in 1984, 1980, and 1962, respectively.

OPPOSITE: Jackie Robinson at bat, 1955. Robinson was the first African American to play in the major leagues, breaking the color barrier in 1947. That year he also was the National League's Rookie of the Year. The Dodgers retired his number 42 in 1972. Major league baseball retired his number in 1997, fifty years after he ended segregation in professional baseball; he is the only player to receive such an honor.

Hank Bauer, Tom Sturdivant, and Mickey Mantle in the locker room after winning Game 4. Sturdivant was the winning pitcher and Mantle and Bauer both hit home runs. The Dodgers and the Yankees met for a rematch in the 1956 World Series, with the Yankees taking back the championship in seven games.

OPPOSITE: Sal Maglie pitching for the Dodgers, and Andy Carey leading off first base while Gil Hodges covers, 1956.

Mickey Mantle stealing second base, with Pee Wee Reese applying the late tag. Mantle is safe, 1956.

Game 5 of the 1956 World Series, Mantle rounding third base in the fourth inning after hitting a home run that would break a scoreless tie. Third-base coach Frank Crosetti (No. 2) is in the foreground, and Jackie Robinson can only watch as Mantle goes by.

Mickey Mantle chasing a fly ball. In the top of the fifth inning of the fifth game, Brooklyn's Gil Hodges hit deep into left-center, Yankee Stadium's own "Death Valley," but his effort was thwarted by a brilliant running catch by Mantle, in what has become known simply as "The Catch," one of several close plays that preserved Don Larsen's perfect game.

Batting left-handed, Mickey hits a home run in Game 4. He also had
home runs in Games 1 and 5.

Don Larsen pitching his perfect game in Game 5 of the 1956 World Series. A perfect game is achieved when a pitcher pitches nine innings with no hits, no walks, no batters hit by a pitch, no batters reaching base for any reason—that is, all players of the opposing team are retired in order. In the history of major-league baseball there have been only 17 perfect games pitched, and Larsen's is the only perfect game and no-hitter in postseason play. His perfect game is one of the most memorable achievements in the history of the World Series.

Yankee Stadium erupts after the third strike is called for the third out in the ninth inning, and Yogi Berra leaps into Larsen's arms at the end of the perfect game.

The fans celebrating on the field after Game 5 at Yankee Stadium. The scoreboard with its fateful row of zeroes tells the story. Larsen would be named MVP of the series for his achievement.

The gentlemen of the press mingle with the players at batting practice before a game.

1957-1958 World Series vs. Milwaukee Braves

Warren Spahn and Whitey Ford are arguably the greatest left-handed pitchers of the era and they met each other on the major battlefield twice—in two seven-game World Series. Spahn and Ford danced together for the first time in 1957's first game. Sad to say, Spahn was chased in the sixth inning (full disclosure: Spahn is my favorite hero of all-time. I wore a Warren Spahn glove that served me well in softball games through my adult years). And so Ford drew first blood.

In Game 4, Spahn pitched against Tom Sturdivant. He took a 4–1 advantage into the ninth inning, thanks to early home runs by Hank Aaron and Frank Torre (Joe's brother). He retired the first two batters, but then gave up singles to Yogi Berra and Gil McDougald, and Elston Howard blasted a three-run home run that tied the game. In the top of the tenth, Spahn still on the mound, Hank Bauer tripled in the go-ahead Yankee run. But in the bottom of the tenth, Braves' shortstop Johnny Logan doubled in the tying run. And Eddie Mathews, their great third baseman, hit what they now call a "walk-off" home run off reliever Bob Grim to win the game 7–5 for the Braves. It must be said that Spahn did allow 11 hits in the game, but his manager, Fred Haney, stayed with his best-loved southpaw. In Game 5, Whitey Ford allowed the Yankees just 1 run and 6 hits, but Lew Burdette, the Yankee killer of 1957, shut them out, 1–0. The Yankees won the sixth game to tie the series. Warren Spahn was supposed to have pitched Game 7, but he came down with the flu. Lew Burdette, pitching with two day's rest, shut out the Yankees, 5–0. And the Braves won its first World Series since 1914.

Spahn and Ford hooked up three times in the closely matched 1958 series. Spahn beat Ford, who was relieved in the eighth inning, 4–3. In Game 4, Ford held the Braves to one run in seven innings, but was outpitched by Spahn, a brilliant 2–0, two-hit shutout. Now the Braves needed only one more victory to beat the Yankees for another World Championship. Bob Turley rescued the Yankees in Game 5 with a 7–0 shutout against the Braves hot starter, Lew Burdette. With only two days' rest, Ford and Spahn went after each other again. Whitey lasted only the first inning. Spahn went all the way to the tenth inning when Gil McDougald hit a lead-off homer to tie the game. Spahn got two out but also allowed two more hits. He was relieved by Don McMahon. Bill Skowron singled in another run. It was 4–2, Yankees. In the last of the tenth the Braves scored a run with two out and Braves on first and third. The Yankees called on Bob Turley to get the final out. He did. Game 7 was tied 2–2 until the seventh inning when Bill Skowron's home run drove in his fifth, sixth, and seventh run of the series off of the once feared Lew Burdette. The other Yankee hero was Bob Turley, who had saved the sixth game. He came in relief of Don Larsen in the third inning and pitched the rest of the game. With Turley and Skowron's help, Casey Stengel won his seventh World Series.

In his career, Whitey Ford won 236 games for the Yankees, lost only 106 lifetime, a .690 win-loss percentage that was the highest reported by any pitcher since 1900. As Casey Stengel put it about Ford, "If you had one game to win and your life depended on it, you'd want him to pitch it."

Warren Spahn's lifetime record, starting in 1942 and ending in 1965, is simply astonishing. He won 363 major-league games, the most ever by a left-handed pitcher. He won 20 games or more in 13 seasons. He also led all National League pitchers in hitting home runs: 35.

Spectators fill the upper deck at Yankee Stadium; an all-American, red-white-and-blue bunting hangs in festive array. The defending champions, the New York Yankees, will have home-field advantage against the Milwaukee Braves in the 1957 series, but the Braves will defeat the Yankees in seven games.

Yogi Berra warming up a pitcher.

OPPOSITE PAGE: Third baseman Andy Carey of the Yankees, 1957. He had a critical RBI in Game 1, to help the Yankees take the first game of the series.

Lew Burdette pitching for the Braves, Elston Howard at bat, in Game 5 at Yankee Stadium, 1958. After a win in Game 2, Burdette would lose Games 5 and 7.

Lew Burdette dominated the 1957 series with three complete game victories in Games 2, 5, and 7, and was named the series MVP. Milwaukee won the series in seven games.

Hank Aaron hitting for the Braves. In the 1957 series, he led both teams with a series average of .393 and 3 home runs and 7 RBIs. The future Hall of Famer (elected in 1982) would cap off an extraordinary career as a 24-time All-Star, the 1957 National League MVP, and 3-time Gold Glove winner, by breaking Babe Ruth's record of 714 career home runs in 1974. He would extend the record to 755 before retiring in 1976.

Hank Bauer played for the Yankees from 1948 to 1959. He won seven World Series championships as a player with the Yankees, and he would go on to win an eighth as manager of the Baltimore Orioles in 1966. He had two great series against the Braves, hitting 2 home runs and 6 RBIs in 1957, and 4 home runs and 8 RBIs in 1958.

Eddie Mathews, third baseman for the Braves.
He was elected to the Hall of Fame in 1978,
and his number 41 was retired by the Braves.

Bob Turley pitching for the Yankees. Turley played for five different major-league baseball teams. He was with the Yankees from 1955 to 1962. Nineteen fifty-eight was his great year, winning 21 games and losing only seven. In the 1958 World Series, he lost Game 2, but went on to win Games 5 and 7, and was credited with a save in Game 6. He was named the series MVP. He also won the Cy Young Award and was named the American League Pitcher of the Year.

Second baseman Gil McDougald at bat. In the 1958 series against
the Braves he had 2 home runs and 4 RBIs.

Warren Spahn pitching for the Braves. The left-hander was one of the great pitchers in baseball history. He pitched to a 1–1 record in the 1957 series—the year he won the Cy Young Award, and a 2–1 record in the 1958 series. He was a four-time National League Pitcher of the Year and the Braves would retire his number (No. 21). He was elected to the Baseball Hall of Fame in 1973.

Eddie Mathews is considered one of the great third basemen in baseball history. He played for the Braves in Boston, Milwaukee, and Atlanta, from 1952 to 1966, and would manage the team from 1972 to 1974.

Whitey Ford was the Yankees Game 1 pitcher in
World Series play from 1955 to 1958 and 1961 to
1964. He won the opening game of the 1957 series
but ended with a 1–1 record, losing in Game 5.

Mantle takes a big swing. Mantle's bat was on fire in the series against Pittsburgh, hitting a .400 average, 3 home runs, and 11 RBIs.

1960
World Series
vs. Pittsburgh Pirates

We've talked plenty about Bill Mazeroski, and the iconic photograph showing the home run and everything around it in all its glory (page 120). What else is there to talk about in the seven-game series except that it cost Casey Stengel his job? Well, for one, it was a ferocious hitting series, especially for the Yankees. In each of their three wins, the Yankees scored in double figures. The big Yankee guns were Mickey Mantle, batting .400, with 10 hits, including 3 home runs and 11 runs batted in; Bill Skowron batting .375 with 12 hits, 2 home runs, and 6 runs batted in. But the Yankees' real hero was second baseman Bobby Richardson, batting .367 with 11 hits and a World Series record 12 runs batted in. For the Pirates, the marvelous Roberto Clemente had 9 hits. The Pirates' first baseman, Rocky Nelson, also had 9 hits, including a homer. And Mazeroski had 8 hits, 5 runs batted in, and 2 home runs. Pirates' pitching held on strongly, too. Harvey Haddix won two games, one in relief. Vern Law also won two games with the help of Roy Face, who saved three games in the series.

All these neat performances left Ed Fitzgerald, the editor of *Sport* magazine, in a quandary. Since the early 1950s, *Sport* had selected the Most Valuable Player of the series, and given that person a flashy Corvette automobile. It was up to Fitzgerald and his cohorts to figure out who deserved the 1960 award most. Bill Mazeroski was the obvious choice of course. Fitzgerald was also looking at Vern Law, who had won two games, and Elroy Face, who had saved three games. Then, of course, from the losing team, there was Skowron, Mantle, and Bobby Richardson. But the magazine had never given the award to a player from a losing team. Fitzgerald gave the car to Bobby Richardson.

No sooner had the victorious Pirates heard about the choice, there was clamor in their dressing room. It was said that Roy Face wanted to come right over to the Yankees' quarters and lay one on Fitzgerald's chin; not because *he* hadn't won the car, but because Bill Mazeroski hadn't won it. Many of the sportswriters felt the same way. But Fitzgerald stuck to his guns.

I have to confess that I was bothered at the time, because I would be replacing Fitzgerald as editor of *Sport* (he would be going on to an important book publishing career) and would be heavily involved in the next MVP award. I'm happy to tell you that in my twelve years as editor of *Sport*, I had never, to my knowledge, been the target of assault by a major-league baseball player.

Mickey Mantle crosses the plate after hitting a home run.

OPPOSITE: At Forbes Field in Pittsburgh, Roberto Clemente (No. 21) takes a long lead off of first base with Yankee first baseman Bill Skowron covering. Clemente played his entire major-league career with Pittsburgh. He was a 12-time All-Star, a 12-time Gold Glove award winner, and a 2-time World Series champion. He was MVP of the 1971 World Series, the year he also won the Babe Ruth Award. He was elected to the Baseball Hall of Fame in 1973, one year after his tragic death in a plane crash while bringing emergency relief to earthquake-stricken Nicaragua.

Vernon Law pitching. Law played for the Pirates his entire career, from 1950–1951 and 1954–1967. 1960 was his best year: he won the Cy Young Award and was named the National League Pitcher. He also was the winning pitcher of Games 1 and 4 on the way to the Pirates World Series championship that year.

Yogi Berra at bat. The Yankee batters were all hitting well in the series. Berra had a .318 average and 8 RBIs himself, and the Yankees overall had an average of .338 and a total of 55 runs scored as compared to Pittsburgh's overall average of .257 and 27 runs scored. But their fate would hinge on Mazeroski's momentous last at bat.

Pirate Harvey Haddix was the winning pitcher of Games 5 and 7.

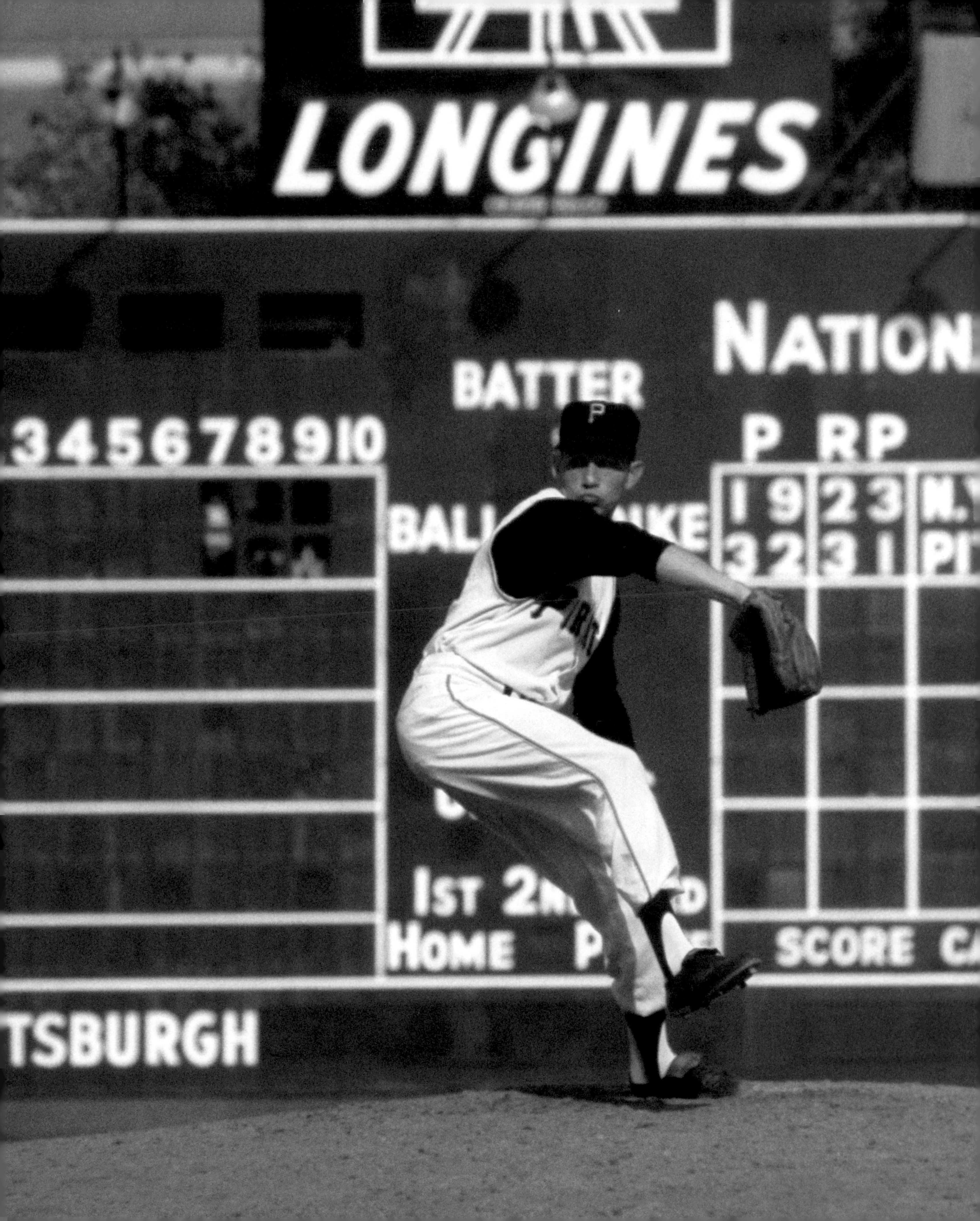
LONGINES
BATTER
3 4 5 6 7 8 9 10
P RP
HOME
SCORE

Rocky Nelson crossing home plate after hitting a home run in Game 7. He is greeted at the plate by Roberto Clemente.

Relief pitcher Bobby Shantz gets a save in Game 2. He also pitched in Games 4 and 7.

Ralph Terry throws to Bill Skowron attempting
to pick off Bill Virdon at first base.

Casey Stengel takes out pitcher Bob Turley in Game 2. Pittsburgh had taken the first game of the series, but the Yankees came back strong in Game 2, to win 16–3. Bob Turley, the winning pitcher, was relieved by Bobby Shantz in the ninth inning.

Bill Mazeroski, the Pirates' second baseman. He played his entire career for the Pittsburgh Pirates, from 1956 to 1972, and was twice a World Series champion, in 1960 and again in 1971. He won the Babe Ruth Award in 1960 and in his career, he won 8 Gold Glove titles and was on 7 All-Star teams. He was elected to the Baseball Hall of Fame in 2001.

"The shot heard 'round the world," captured in one of the most famous baseball photographs ever. The devastating walk-off home run by Bill Mazeroski, at the bottom of the ninth inning of Game 7 of the 1960 World Series in Forbes Field in Pittsburgh, was the first ever to win a World Series. The Yankees had dominated the Pirates in every aspect of the game, but had not been able to put them away, and suddenly they were vanquished. The ball is seen on the rise and to the right of the clock.

The crowd rushes to surround Mazeroski, while Casey Stengel, in the lower left corner, looks on.

Stengel says good-bye to the New York Yankees. After the disappointing loss to Pittsburgh, the Yankee management fired Stengel. In his twelve years as manager of the New York Yankees, from 1949 to 1960, he had won 7 World Series titles and 10 American League pennants. He would go on to manage the other New York team, the Mets, from 1962 to 1965.

Bill Skowron at bat in Cincinnati. In the 1961
World Series against the Cincinnati Reds,
the Yankees got back into their winning
form. Skowron hit a home run in Game 1 at
Yankee Stadium. The first baseman played
for the team from 1954 to 1962 when he
was traded away to the Dodgers.

1961 World Series vs. Cincinnati Reds

First, I want to be clear that no one threatened my life when *Sport* gave the Corvette to Whitey Ford as the 1961 MVP of the World Series. As I have noted, Ford, ably abetted by the offense, pitched two shutouts against the Pirates in 1960, 12–0 and 10–0. And here, in this most glorious year for the Yankees, Ford pitched two more shutouts, a 2–0 win in Game 1, and 7–0 in Game 4. The Yankees won the fifth game, closing out the series. During the regular season, Whitey compiled a 25–4 record. He led the league in innings pitched, 283, and his pitching percentage of .862 was the highest of any Yankee pitcher in history. His 210 strikeouts were also the most of any left-handed Yankee pitcher in history. And, of course, Whitey won the Cy Young Award for the year. But let me not forget Luis Arroyo, the best relief pitcher in the league in '61. He appeared in 65 games while assembling a 15–5 record. To me, Ford and Arroyo were bookends for a team that I believe to be the greatest Yankee team ever.

A majority of baseball experts, however, tend to call the 1927 Yankees the best of all time. One of them was Phil Rizzuto in his 1962 book, *The 'Miracle' New York Yankees*. But he felt it was very close. "Despite Ruth and Gehrig," Rizzuto wrote, "the '27 club did not have the brute power of the '61 team. Babe Ruth hit his 61 home runs, Lou Gehrig hit 47. Mantle and Maris became the first club from the same team to top Ruth and Gehrig; in 1927 that dynamic duo hit 107 home runs. Mickey and Roger hit 115."

Let's look at other statistics. The Yankees hit more home runs in a single year, 240, than any other team in the history of baseball. The Yankees set the major-league record for most games won at home, 65; they also set the record for the most pinch-hit home runs for one club in a season. Oh, and also, the '61 Yankees were the first team in baseball to have six players hit 20 or more home runs—Maris 61, Mantle 54, Skowron 28, Berra 22, Howard 21, and Blanchard 21.

To give the 1927 Yankees their due, they did win 110 games, while the '61 Yankees won only 109. That year Roger Maris won the MVP, Ford won the Cy Young Award, and Luis Arroyo was the best relief pitcher, appearing in 65 games while assembling a 15–5 record with a 2.19 earned run average.

The Yankees were at the peak of their dynasty that had begun twelve years back. How much longer could it last?

Elio Chacón called safe at home plate. He scored the winning run in
the Reds' only victory against the Yankees in Game 2.

Joey Jay pitching for Cincinnati. A 21–10 pitcher that season, he pitched the winning Game 2 for the Reds.

Roger Maris hitting. The year 1961 was the season of home runs for the Yankees. Mantle and Maris were in a duel as to who would take Babe Ruth's record of 60 home runs in a season, until September when Mantle was injured. Mantle would end the season with 54 home runs to Maris's record-breaking 61 home runs, the last of which was achieved on the last day of the regular season. Four other Yankee players had hit over 20 home runs that season, for a team record of 240 home runs in the season. During the series Maris added a home run to his tally in Game 3.

Mickey Mantle batting left-handed. When Mantle was first observed playing in a semi-professional game by a Yankee scout, he hit two big home runs, one left-handed and one right-handed. In his major-league career, he would go on to hit 372 left-handed home runs and 164 right-handed. Despite the variance, Mantle thought he was a better hitter right-handed than left. The number of right-handed pitchers he faced and the configuration of Yankee Stadium combined to favor his left-hand side.

Wally Post's home run in the fifth inning of Game 5 in Cincinnati.

Frank Robinson batting in Yankee Stadium. He had hit 37 home runs in the regular season and was the National League's MVP, but he would knock in only 1 home run, in Game 5, in the series. He would have better success in the World Series in 1966 and 1970 with the Baltimore Orioles. He was a player on five major-league teams and a manager of four teams. He was elected to the Baseball Hall of Fame in 1982.

Gordy Coleman's home run for Cincinnati in Game 2. In all, the Reds hit only 3 home runs and 11 RBIs to the Yankees 7 home runs and 26 RBIs.

Coleman leaping for first base with Bill Skowron covering.

OPPOSITE: Yankee shortstop Tony Kubek. He played his entire career with the Yankees, from 1957 to 1965, but was cut short with a back injury. He was Rookie of the Year in 1957 and a three-time World Series champion.

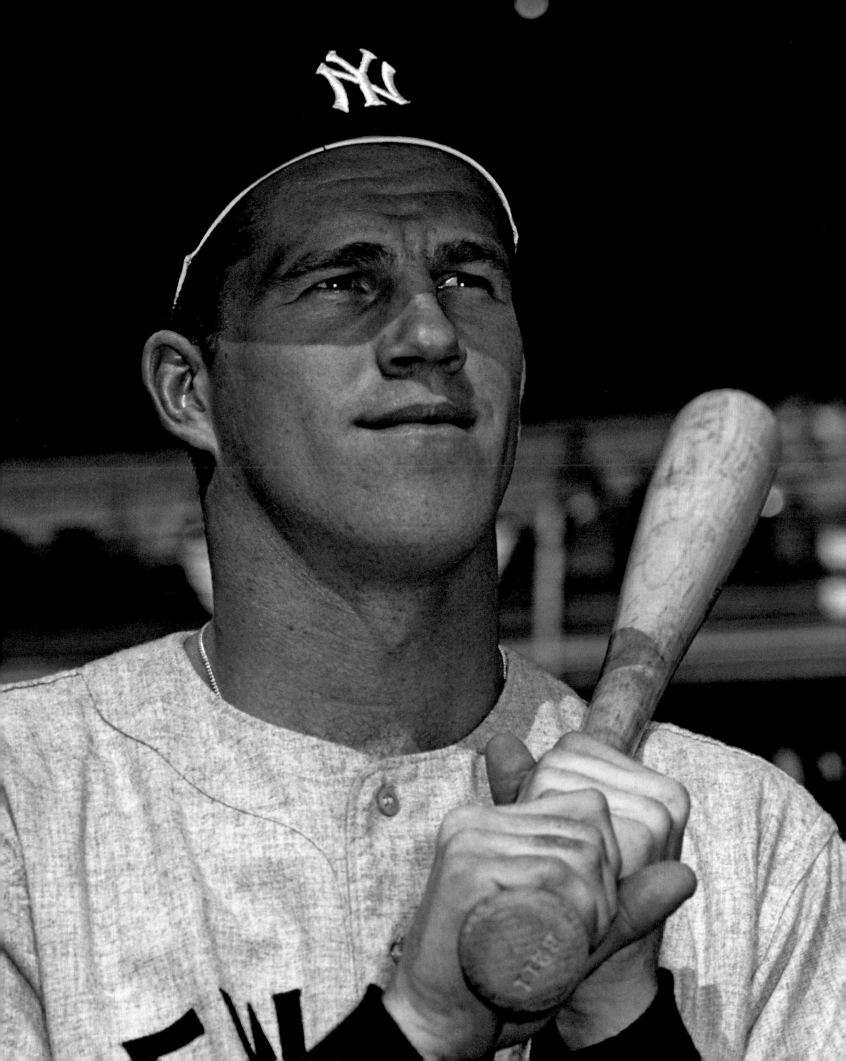

A successful pickoff at first base.

Yogi Berra hits a home run in Game 2. He is greeted at home plate by Johnny Blanchard (No. 38), Roger Maris, and the bat boy. The Yankees took the series in five games.

Willie Mays at bat. Except for his last year with the Mets, Mays played his entire career with the New York and San Francisco Giants. One of the greatest all-around players in the history of the game, Mays has been heaped with honors, but he won only one World Series title (in 1954). He was elected to the Hall of Fame in 1979.

1962 World Series
vs. San Francisco Giants

The San Francisco Giants had no time to prepare for a World Series. They were suddenly locked in an intense pennant race with the Los Angeles Dodgers who seemed the likely opponents for the Yankees that year. But, the Dodgers lost to the Cardinals, and the fourth playoff in National League history would start the next day. In the third and final game, Maury Wills, the Dodgers' shortstop, hit 4 singles and stole 2 bases, his 103rd and 104th. (He would be named MVP of the year in the National League.) Wills, however, couldn't do it all. The Giants, scoring 4 runs in the ninth, beat the Dodgers 6–4. The Yankees were going to San Francisco.

In Game 1, Whitey Ford allowed 10 hits but the Yankees won, 6–2. The series would not be an easy one for the Yankees. In Game 2, the Giants' Jack Sanford, who had won 24 games in the season, pitched a 2–0 shutout, helped by a Willie McCovey home run. In Game 3, Bill Stafford of the Yankees beat Billy Pierce, 3–2. But the Giants came right back in Game 4, with second baseman Chuck Hiller hitting a grand slam home run in the top of the seventh. The Giants won it 7–3. The winning pitcher for SF? Who else but Don Larsen? The Yankees took their turn in Game 5, Ralph Terry fashioning a strong 5–3 victory. Then it rained and rained. Three days later the teams got back on the field. Billy Pierce pitched a beautiful game, allowing the Yankees but 2 runs and 3 hits. One of those hits was a home run by Roger Maris. And so it was down to the seventh game: Ralph Terry vs. Jack Sanford. This is when I started to think, who in God's name can be the MVP of this series? Both teams had played well, but no Mazeroski had come out of the pack. For the Yankees, Mickey Mantle batted .120. Roger Maris, .174. Yogi Berra

was hurt and only played in two games. Tom Tresh ended up batting .321 with 9 hits and 4 RBIs.

The Giants were in the same condition. Willie Mays batted .250 with 7 hits. Chuck Hiller was a candidate with his big home run and 5 RBIs. If either Jack Sanford or Ralph Terry could win his second game in this game of games, he'd be a contender. It turned out that both pitchers were magnificent. It was the Yankees, 1–0, as the last of the ninth opened. The first batter was pinch-hitter Matty Alou. He threw down a bunt single. Terry struck out the next two hitters, but he couldn't get Willie Mays out. Mays doubled to right. Alou was a fast runner and might have scored but Roger Maris gunned a lifesaving throw into the infield and Alou had to hold on third. Up strode Willie McCovey. He had homered off Terry in the second game. Ralph must have remembered that he was the one who threw the ball that Mazeroski put away. McCovey was trouble. McCovey swung at the third pitch Terry had given him. He hit a screamer of a line drive headed for the outfield. I immediately saw who my MVP would be, except that second baseman Bobby Richardson was there and the ball stung into his glove, and it was all over.

In the Yankees dressing room, Ralph Houk accepted a glass of champagne, becoming the fifth manager to have won a World Series on his first and second tries. Ralph Terry was near his locker, surrounded by the press. He was the series MVP and would shortly be the owner of a bright red Corvette. He smiled in delight.

Thus ended 1962, the Yankees winning a World Championship that would be especially cherished. It was their last one for fifteen years.

ABOVE: Yankee second baseman Bobby Richardson throwing and San Francisco Giant Orlando Cepeda sliding in a double play.

BELOW: A Yankee slides home while Bill Skowron (#14) watches from the on deck circle and pitcher Jack Sanford looks for a throw.

Ralph Terry pitching for the Yankees. He lost
Game 2, but came back to win Games 5 and 7.

First baseman Orlando Cepeda played for the Giants from 1958 to 1966. In 1961 he had hit 46 home runs and 142 RBIs. The Giants would outplay the Yankees in many key areas, but they would not succeed in taking the title from the defending champions.

Jack Sanford pitching for the Giants. Sanford had a regular season
record of 24–7 and 3.43 E.R.A, and he was the winning pitcher in Game
2, with Ralph Terry the losing pitcher. However, the situation would
reverse in both Games 5 and 7, with Terry winning and Sanford losing.

Willie Mays, "the Say Hey Kid," connects, Johnny Blanchard catching. Blanchard holds the record for most World Series pinch hits at 10, and he is tied for the most hits by a pinch hitter in the World Series at 3.

Willie Mays rounding third, waved in by the third-base coach. This
was his last appearance in the World Series as a Giant.

Yankee third baseman Clete Boyer hit a home run in Game 1. A strong defensive player on a team of hitters, Boyer nonetheless led the team with a batting average of .318, and had 4 RBIs in the series.

Giants pitcher Billy Pierce after winning a complete-game three-hitter in Game 6.

Roger Maris crossing home plate. The new single season home run record holder was not as masterful in the series, but he did hit 1 home run and 5 RBIs, and he scored 4 times.

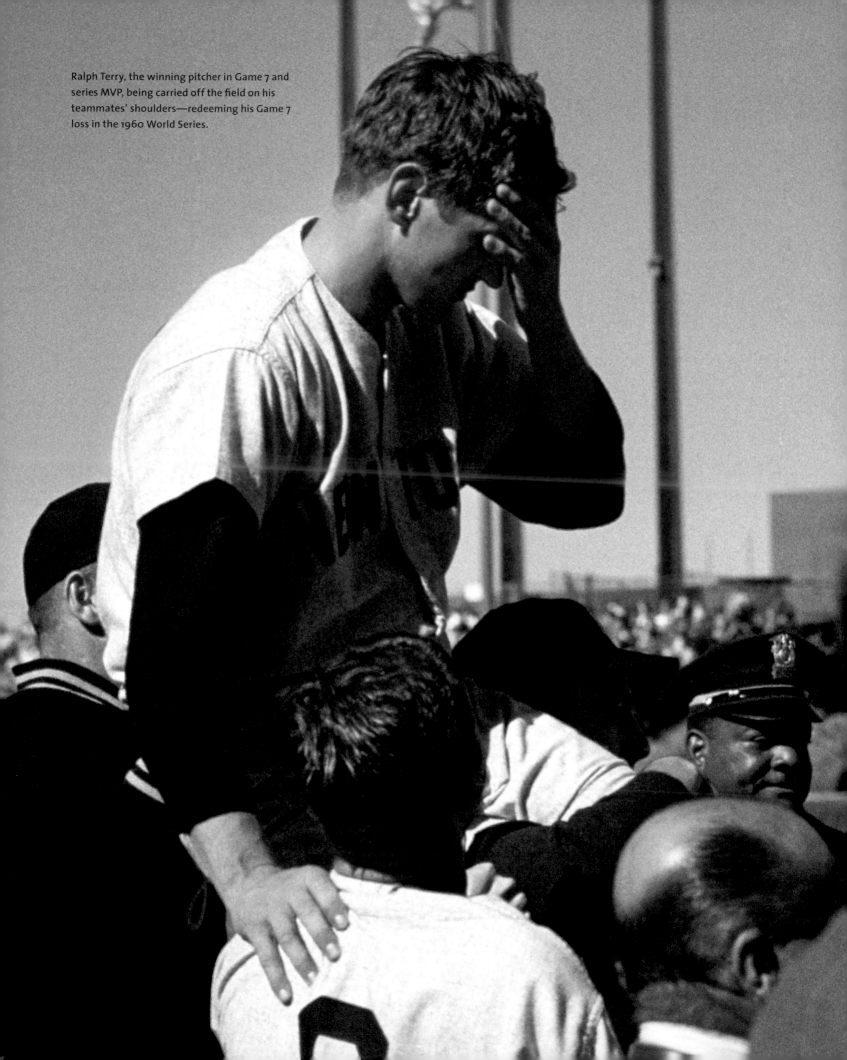

Ralph Terry, the winning pitcher in Game 7 and series MVP, being carried off the field on his teammates' shoulders—redeeming his Game 7 loss in the 1960 World Series.

Manager Ralph Houk, reaching for a proffered glass of champagne, celebrates in the locker room after beating the San Francisco Giants four games to two. In his second year as manager for the Yankees, he led the team to a second World Series title.

Managers Ralph Houk and Walter Alston before the cameras. As a player for the Yankees from 1947 to 1954, Houk had been a backup catcher to Yogi Berra. He made the transition to manager working in the minor leagues and then as Casey Stengel's first base coach from 1958 to 1960. Alston was named manager of the Brooklyn Dodgers in 1954 and led the team to its only World Series title in 1955. After the team moved to Los Angeles, he would guide them to three more World Series victories in 1959, 1963, and 1965.

1963
World Series
vs. Los Angeles Dodgers

After winning the American League pennant by 10 ½ games, the New York Yankees came into the World Series at the wrong time, and they were swept away. The sweeper was Sandy Koufax, in the middle of his extraordinary career, when he was virtually untouchable. During the '63 season he won 25 games. Twenty of his twenty-five wins were complete games, eleven of them were shutouts. His earned run average was 1.88. He was primed for this series. In Game 1, Koufax struck out the first five Yankees he faced, ending up with a record-breaking 15 strikeouts. He beat Whitey Ford in that first game, 5–2.

Johnny Podres came back to haunt the Yankees once again, winning a 4–1 decision in Game 2. Don Drysdale did it in Game 3 in a close one. Jim Bouton allowed the Dodgers only 1 run and 3 hits, but Drysdale shut out the Yankees, 1–0, allowing them only 3 hits. And here was Koufax, back in Game 4, pitching a six-hitter, putting away the Yankees for good, 2–1.The Yankee run was a home run by Mickey Mantle. It was certainly the Yankees worst effort ever in the life of their dynasty. The Yankees wound up batting .171 as a team. They scored only 4 runs, the second lowest total in World Series history. Now we know why Dodger manager Walter Alston was poking a finger at Ralph Houk in Marvin Newman's close-up of the two. Houk was moving up to general manager and Yogi Berra would be the new manager. The one other good thing that happened to the Yankees that year was that Elston Howard won the MVP Award.

Mickey Mantle and Whitey Ford before a game.

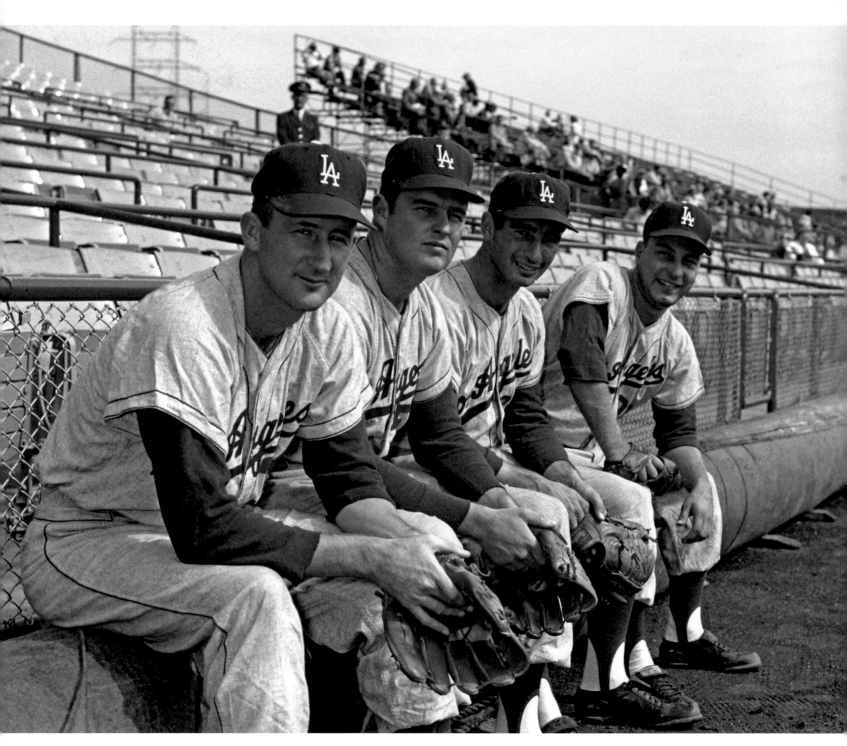

Pitchers for the Dodgers, from left to right; Roger Craig, Don Drysdale, Sandy Koufax, and Johnny Podres. Craig was not on the team in 1963, but the other three, along with reliever Ron Perranoski, swept the Yankees.

Ron Perranoski earned a save in Game 2, coming in to relieve
winning pitcher Johnny Podres. It was a game that also saw former
Yankee Bill Skowron hit a home run in the fourth inning.

Shortstop Maury Wills, one of the fastest men in baseball, gets a
leadoff hit. During the 1963 season he stole 40 bases.

Sandy Koufax. His name is synonymous with strikeouts. He spent his entire career with the Brooklyn/Los Angeles Dodgers, from 1955 to 1966. In 1963 he won his first of three pitcher's Triple Crowns, leading the league, in fact, both leagues, in wins (25), strikeouts (306), and E.R.A (1.88). He also pitched 11 shutouts that season. He won the Cy Young Award and was named the National League MVP and, winning Games 1 and 4 of the World Series, he was named the series MVP. His 15 strikeouts in Game 1 broke the World Series record. He would retire from baseball in 1966 and become the youngest player elected to the Baseball Hall of Fame in 1972.

Pitcher Jim Bouton warming up before Game 3, which he would lose to Don Drysdale. Bouton would later write the controversial *Ball Four*, a book deemed "detrimental to baseball" by Commissioner Bowie Kuhn. Behind-the-scenes revelations and references to Mickey Mantle's lifestyle resulted in his being effectively ostracized by the Yankee organization and baseball in general. Mantle and Bouton reconciled in the 1990s and the Yankees invited Bouton to his first Old Timers' Day at Yankee Stadium in 1998, sadly it was also Joe DiMaggio's last.

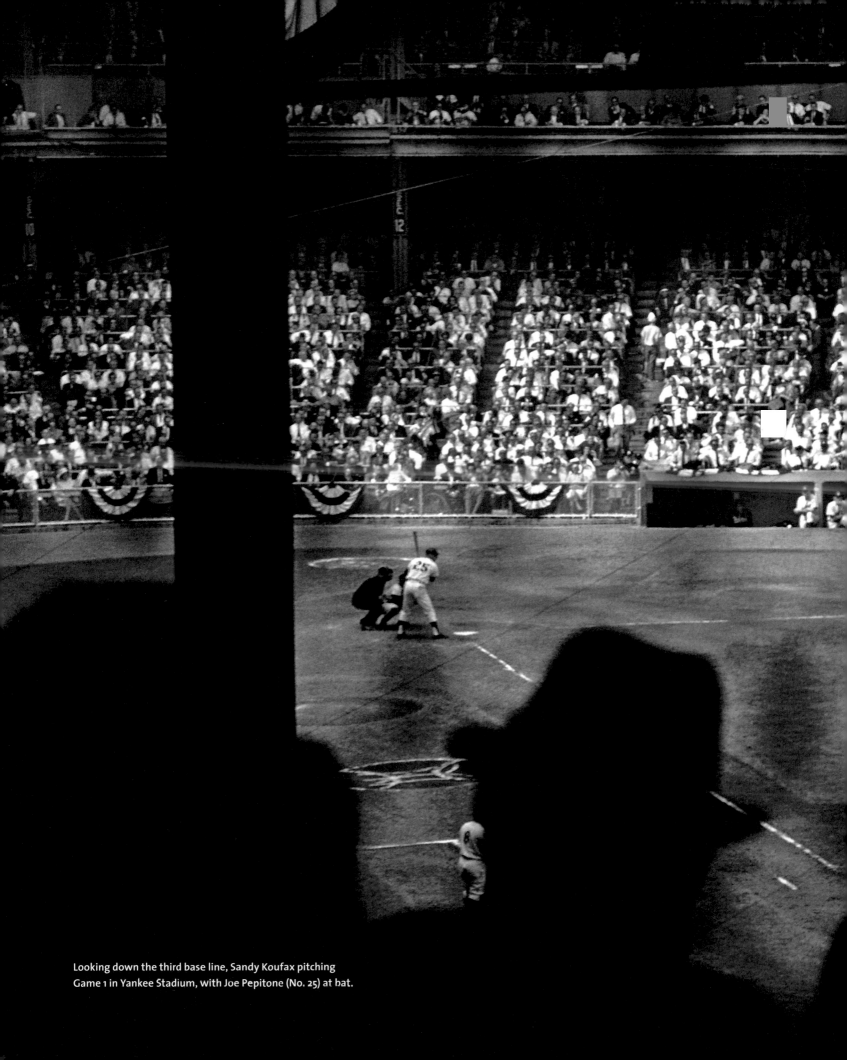

Looking down the third base line, Sandy Koufax pitching
Game 1 in Yankee Stadium, with Joe Pepitone (No. 25) at bat.

Jim Gilliam crosses home plate, congratulated by Maury Wills. Elston Howard (No. 32) is the catcher.

The Los Angeles dugout as Dick Tracewski (#44) is being congratulated by manager Walter Alston, coach Leo Durocher, and his teammates for scoring a run.

Yankee fans on the field in Yankee Stadium. The two-time defending World Series champions had home field advantage, but lost in four games to the Dodgers. The powerful pitching of the Dodgers gave up only 4 runs to the Yankees in the series. Here Yankee fans in a somber mood file onto the field, as if to pay homage to the passing of an era.

Bob Gibson pitching for the Cardinals. Gibson, the greatest pitcher in the history of the St. Louis Cardinals, lost Game 2, but came back to win Games 5 and 7, overpowering the Yankees. He would be elected to the Baseball Hall of Fame in 1981.

1964 World Series vs. St. Louis Cardinals

Gee, the Yankees got stuck for the second year in a row. Sandy Koufax last year, Bob Gibson this one. But they fought the Cardinals down to the wire. St. Louis had a great team. They had Lou Brock, the most accomplished base runner in baseball (see Marvin Newman's masterly shot of Brock flying). They had Ken Boyer, who would win the MVP in '64, playing against his brother Clete. They had Curt Flood, a fleet center fielder, and catcher Tim McCarver, who batted .478 in this World Series, with 11 hits and 5 RBIs. For the Yankees it was Mickey Mantle, playing his best World Series ever. Mickey batted .333, with 8 hits, 3 home runs, and 6 runs batted in. And the Yankees battled all the way. The Cardinals won the first game 9–5, with Whitey Ford pitching five good innings before Curt Flood's RBI triple in the sixth inning. Yankee rookie Mel Stottlemyre won the second game beating Bob Gibson 8–3. Jim Bouton pitched a saucy third game, beating the Cardinals 2–1. Mantle struck the decisive home run. In Game 4, Ken Boyer's bases-loaded home run was all the Cardinals needed in the 4–3 victory. In Game 5, Gibson outpitched Mel Stottlemyre to win, 6–5. Bouton and Curt Simmons pitched Game 6, and it was like old times. In the sixth inning Mantle and Maris hit back-to-back home runs. Bouton got the win in the 8–3 game. Bob Gibson didn't pitch the game of his life in the finale, but even with homers by Mantle and Clete Boyer (his brother also hit a home run in the game), Gibson outlasted them all. In the series, he struck out 31 Yankees, a World Series record at the time.

Yankee management couldn't wait. They fired Yogi Berra a day after the Cardinals' victory. The great reference book on baseball, *Total Baseball*, said of the Yankees, "When the Series was over, the long era of Yankee dominance had come to an end." And they were right.

Cardinals and Yankees on the field at batting practice before a game, with groundskeepers silhouetted in the foreground.

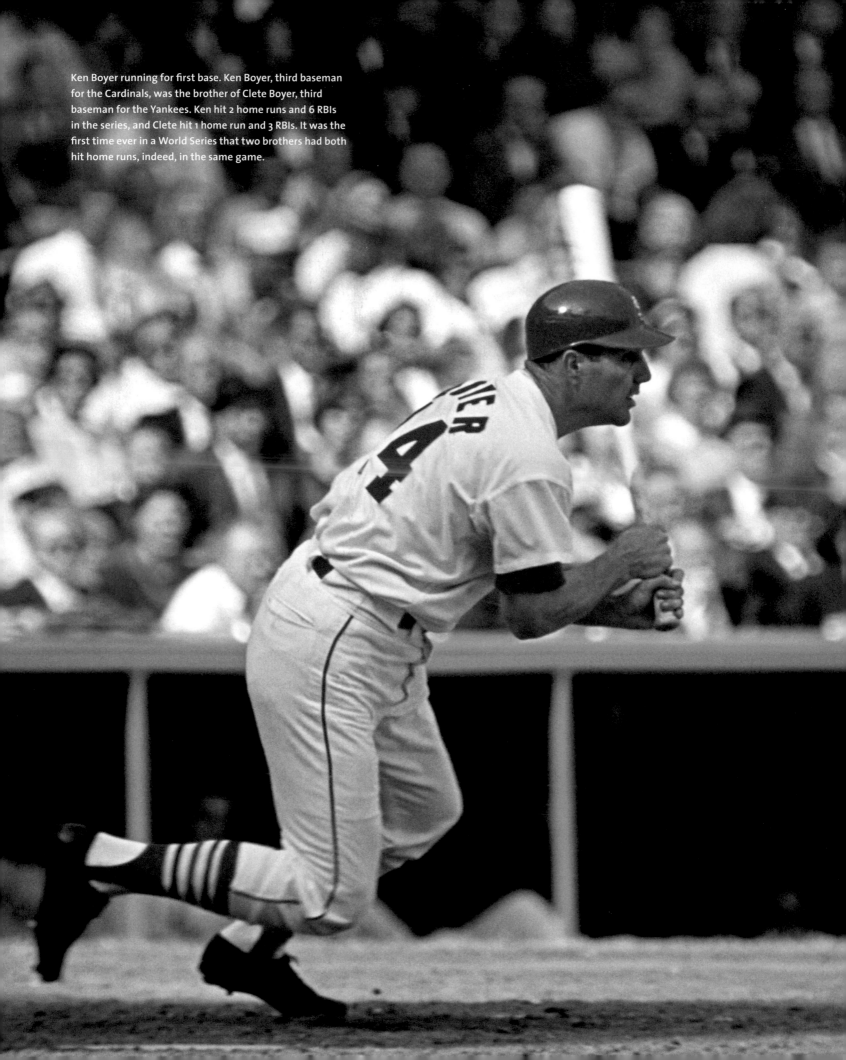

Ken Boyer running for first base. Ken Boyer, third baseman for the Cardinals, was the brother of Clete Boyer, third baseman for the Yankees. Ken hit 2 home runs and 6 RBIs in the series, and Clete hit 1 home run and 3 RBIs. It was the first time ever in a World Series that two brothers had both hit home runs, indeed, in the same game.

Mel Stottlemyre pitching for the Yankees. Playing in his rookie year, Stottlemyre would win Game 2, defeating Bob Gibson.

Elston Howard at bat, and running for first base.

Bob Gibson at the start of his wind up.

Bob Gibson was nursing a two-run lead in the ninth inning of Game 5 with two outs when Tom Tresh hit a two-run homer to ward off defeat until McCarver's three-run blast in the tenth inning gave the game to Gibson. Tresh also hit a home run in Game 1.

Future broadcaster Tim McCarver hits a three-run homer in the
tenth inning to win Game 5.

Lou Brock at bat, and (following spread) running for first base. The future Hall of Famer (elected in 1985) hit a home run in the fifth inning of Game 7 leading to a three-run inning and an insurmountable 6–0 lead despite 3 home runs by the Yankees.

Lou Brock running to first, 1964 World Series,
St. Louis Cardinals vs. Yankees.

St. Louis fans cheering their team.

Joe Pepitone hit a grand slam home run in Game 6.

Bob Gibson would come back from his loss in Game 2 to defeat the Yankee pitcher Pete Mikkelsen in Game 5, and turn the tables on Stottlemyre in Game 7 to end the series with a 2–1 record and take the series MVP title.

Bob Gibson was named the series MVP. Here, Gibson and Tim McCarver embrace, the Cardinals celebrate, and the great Yankee dynasty of 1949 to 1964—and the Mantle era—come to an end.

Mickey Mantle welcomes Joe DiMaggio at the Old Timers' Day game, 1978.

Old Timers' Day

Isn't it a shame that the Old Timers' Day game is becoming a thing of the past in most major-league cities. On those special days it was wonderful to bring your children to the ballpark and point out the old ballplayers you loved as a young man. The Yankees did a very special thing in the summer of 2008, their last summer under the sunlight of the House that Ruth Built. They brought ballplayers out, and it was both a cheerful and tearful reunion of the gang that used to play the game so well. I think it's a real treat that we're able to see what old-timer afternoons were like from the photos of a legendary summer day in 1978 with the greatest Yankees of an era. Mickey Mantle and Joe DiMaggio were smiling and joking together. When they were playing together in 1951, there was no joking or anything positive going on between the two. DiMaggio, in his last year, wanted to keep his throne, and Mantle was pushing him away, although this was not really true because Mantle didn't yet know where he would fit in the big picture of baseball. So this is a cherished relic of what life could do for both men under different circumstances. And look at that lineup of Yankee greats, front side and back side—Joe DiMaggio, Mickey Mantle, Roger Maris, Billy Martin, Yogi Berra, and Whitey Ford. In the single shots of these men, they all seem relaxed, except for Yogi who perhaps was figuring out a lineup for the game that yesterday's heroes would play. I wonder who's telling the joke in this picture of Berra, Martin, and Maris all looking at Mantle. Could Yogi tell us what did he say?

Whitey Ford. In the World Series record book, the six-time World
Series champion still holds the following records: bases on balls, 34;
games pitched, 22; games started, 22; games started (opening game
of the series), 8; innings pitched,146; losses, 8; strikeouts, 94; and
wins, 10. He won the Cy Young Award and World Series MVP in 1961
and he was a three-time American League Pitcher of the Year.

Yogi Berra in the dugout. A ten-time World Series champion, Yogi Berra still holds the following World Series records: number of at bats, 259; doubles, 10 (tied); hits, 71; home runs, 12 (third, after Babe Ruth); plate appearances, 295; and singles, 49. He was also a three-time American League MVP.

Billy Martin was a five-time World Series champion as a player for the Yankees, and he added a sixth World Series championship as the Yankees' manager in 1977, the year before this picture was taken.

Mickey Mantle smiles for his old pal, the photographer Marvin E. Newman. The seven-time World Series champion Mantle still holds the following World Series records: base on balls, 43; extra base hits, 26; home runs, 18; RBIs, 40; runs scored, 42; strikeouts, 54; and total bases, 123.

From left: Yogi Berra, Billy Martin, Roger Maris, and Mickey Mantle sharing a laugh.

In uniform, from left to right: Whitey Ford (No. 16), Yogi Berra (No. 8), Billy Martin (No. 1), Roger Maris (No. 9), Mickey Mantle (No. 7), and Joe DiMaggio (No. 5)—six of the fifteen numbers retired by the Yankees to honor its players and managers.

Acknowledgments

Marvin Newman would like to thank:

My wife Brigitte, my son, Harrison, and my daughter, Nadja, for their infinite patience and love. Al Silverman, my past partner and longtime friend, for his superb text. Christopher Sweet, who inspired this project. Bruce Silverstein, Elizabeth Shank, and the staff of The Bruce Silverstein Gallery for balancing my two worlds of sports and art. Steve Fine, *Sports Illustrated's* director of photography, who helped continue my relationship with the magazine these past fifty years. Sean Corcoran, the curator at The Museum of the City of New York, for my *Look Magazine* negatives. Yogi Berra for all the insightful memories we both share, and David Kaplan, the director of The Yogi Berra Museum and Learning Center. The publisher of Abrams, Steve Tager, who always understood my special relationship with these Yankees. My editor, Rebecca Isenberg, who made sure we finished on schedule. Our art director Michelle Ishay and José A. Contreras, our designer, whose layouts speak for themselves.

Al Silverman would like to thank:

My wife Rosa and our three Yankee diehards—Tom, Brian, and Matthew, and their three cheerleaders, Donna, Heather, and Nancy.

Index